Career Savvy People Skills

How to ask the Smart Questions for winning the games of career and life.

Michael McGaulley, J.D.
Lawyer & Management Consultant

ISBN-13: 978-0692666166

ISBN-10: 0692666168

Note: ISBN numbers are relevant only to paper editions

Published by Champlain House Media

MichaelMcGaulley.net

SQ B 16 A P P 2

CONTENTS

Your eyes pop open. You look around. You find that you're a pawn on a chessboard.

You're hot and tired and bruised and battered and a little bloodied from the pounding you've been taking.

You push on, you do your best, but you're still knocked off-balance time and again by hits coming from unexpected directions.

You spot an opening, a chance to go for it, to break out of the pack of other hard-working, faceless pawns, to pull off a real success.

Then bang! You're blind-sided. You fell into a trap. It's all over. You're out of the game.

"Why?" you ask yourself. "Why wasn't I smart enough to see this coming? Why didn't I realize what was really going on?"

As we'll be using it in this book, "smart" comes down to abilities like these:

- To be able to look at situations and take in all aspects (and potential problems)—visible and hidden, present, past and what might be coming;

- To spot and stay focused on what is most important;

- To look through confusion and subterfuge, and to spot any games that others might be playing;

- To spot any hidden or covert "players" who may have an interest in the outcome.

- To recognize or generate good potential solutions;

- Ultimately, to choose the best of the options available. . . and to be able to defend that decision.

Introduction:
HOW TO ASK THE SMART QUESTIONS FOR WINNING THE GAMES OF CAREER AND LIFE

"You have to learn the rules of the game. And then you have to play better than anyone else."

Albert Einstein

There are games we play for fun, or for learning, or just to pass the time . . . and *everyone knows* that they *are* games—baseball, chess, soccer, bridge, tennis.

But then there are the *other* kinds of games—secret, covert games that are played (usually on the job), not for fun, but for keeps. Secret games that the opposing players don't tell us are under way, nor what the rules are, nor even what "winning" consists of. (*Sometimes those subtle games do have a name: "office politics"*).

Like it or not, approve of it or not, the reality is that subtle games, probes, and covert competitions are facts of life in most organizations, and you are at a significant disadvantage if you fail to spot them, early-on, and respond appropriately.

This from a federal GS-14, a rising star within the Department, who I interviewed in the course of developing a career development training program:

"You've got to be aware of the games that are being played. You don't have to play the games yourself, but you do need to recognize when they are being played against you.

"One of the classic games is pushing a new person to see where they draw the line. If they're weak, or naive, they give up a lot of ground before they try to draw the boundaries.

"For example, a person might come to you and ask for something that's just a bit borderline. If you're not tuned in to the game, you might let yourself be pressured into saying yes. Then, next time, the request will be a bit further over the border, but you've already established the precedent, and so you give up a bit more.

"You need to start out alert to the game, so you push back and make them really prove their case the first time. If you do that, the chances are they'll back off and say something on the order of, 'I agree with you, but just thought I should run it past you for your reaction.'

"At that point, you've established your credentials. You've shown you can't be fooled. Once you've done that, you won't be likely to get much more trouble."

And this from a friend on spotting and winning the interview game within a *Fortune* Top 50 firm:

"I'd been through the whole hiring sequence: the initial interview, some tests, a follow-up interview with the Branch Manager. Then they called and asked me to come in for what they said would be a brief meeting with the person who would be my actual supervisor. I was given the impression this was just a formality before I was officially offered the job.

"When I got there, we talked a little, and then he said, 'I'm sorry to have to tell you this, but I can see that you're not *quite right for us, after all. I can only apologize for our having taken so much of your time.'*

"I really wanted this job, and was sure that I had it. Now I saw it all falling apart. Then I realized what he was up to, and I said, 'Frankly, I think you'd be making a serious mistake if you don't hire me. Actually, there are several reasons. In the first place . . .'

"After a bit, he laughed and said, 'Congratulations, Mary. You just passed the final test. The job is yours. We just needed to see how you'd handle it. We need people who can think on their feet, and who don't give up.'"

Your work is what puts food on the table and a roof overhead, so your career is definitely *not* just another game. Nevertheless, it's a good idea to look at your work and career as if it *were* a game.

Trouble is, in most cases it's up to you to figure out what that "game" is, along with the real rules of the game as it's played there, and how you excel at the game. After all, knowledge is power, and not all of your associates will be ready to share with someone who may soon be a competitor.

Beyond that, there may be *multiple* games under way, most of them invisible unless you know what to look for.

Double perspective

It's essential to develop a kind of double mental perspective. That is,

- One part of your awareness is down in the fray, doing your job, engaged with the others in the moment;

- But at the same time another aspect of you is the chess player sitting up above the board, viewing the larger picture, looking not just at what *is* happening at this moment, but what else *might* happen, thereby opening up other situations and options.

When you develop that kind of double perspective, you'll begin attuning to elements like these:

- the use of probes, ploys, tests;

- strategic disinformation (i.e. saying or doing things to mislead the opponent on what is really going on);

- pretexting (using cover stories to conceal hidden agendas);

- covert actions (and miscellaneous "sneaky stuff");

- phony emotions—perhaps to "friend" you, perhaps to intimidate you;

- sometimes operating through stand-ins. (Think of *that* the next time the boss asks you to sit in for her at a meeting: Maybe this isn't really a vote of confidence in you, but rather a subtle way of setting you up to take the fire . . . and the fall, if there's problem.)

- And, of course, all the forms and nuances of office politics.

These are just *some* of the types of games and game-elements, all of which you have very likely encountered . . . though you may not have recognized at the time for what they were.

The best way of spotting and decoding these games—as well as of focusing your efforts—is to develop the discipline of asking smart, savvy questions . . . smart questions like those I suggest in this book, questions drawn from my work as a lawyer and management consultant . . . both professions in which developing the ability to cut quickly through a morass of information (and sometimes intentional "disinformation") is essential to success.

The questions

The book is structured around a checklist of 16 "smart questions" that I've found particularly helpful, each in a chapter by itself, along with related secondary questions that will be helpful in arriving at sound answers to the larger questions.

The questions fall into three broad groups:

> *Part one: What is this "Game" About?*

> *Part two: How Am I Doing So Far?*

> *Part three: What's My Best Move at this Point?*

You'll also find other tools, including checklists and templates helpful in making sense of the array of ideas and information. The templates are not forms that must be filled out; rather, they are tools available to use help you.

With the exception of a few items drawn from magazines and other publications (labeled as such), the quotations here are from clients, friends, and other consultants and lawyers, taken from my notes at the time.

> *"Come, Watson, come! The game is afoot!"*

Part one:
WHAT IS THIS "GAME" ABOUT?

"The first step to getting the things you want out of life is this: Decide what you want."

Ben Stein

Part one focuses on the situation you face: the "game," in our terminology. (That game or situation may be a single event, or it may be a pattern spread across months or across a whole job.)

The four questions in Part one are tools for opening through to the core issues.

Question 1 How do *we* "win"? That is, "Where" do we want or need to be afterward, and how will we recognize that we've arrived there?

Question 2 Who else is involved in this "game"? What is likely to be their idea of winning?

Question 3 What's really going on here? Is this a real issue, or a subtle test?

Question 4 What is this situation ultimately about? Where is the crunch?

Note: I'll be using "we" and "I" interchangeably here, as sometimes you'll be operating alone, and other times as part of a team.

Question 1

How do I (my team) "win"? That is, "Where" do we want or need to be afterward, and how will we recognize that we've arrived there?

"If you don't know where you're going, someone else will get there first . . . and eat your lunch."

Unknown

What "winning" means might seem very obvious: To accomplish the objective that you have set for yourself, or that your boss, or your job description, have set for you.

But that's not necessarily all of it. For one thing, that may not be the *correct* objective. Or that objective may be too narrow in scope, not go far enough, or be inclusive enough. That objective, in short, may not really fit what is needed here.

The reality is, it's often not easy to figure what "winning" means in the subtle games within organizations. Typically, a major challenge of these games comes in figuring out *just what that game is really about*—that is, what "winning" means in this situation, to you, *and* to the others involved.

Beyond that, a major part of the "game" may be determining both *who the other players really are*, as well as in getting a sense of *what winning means to each of them*. (The *apparent* players—that is, the *visible* ones—may be obvious enough. But there may also be "hidden" players may be operating through surrogates. And each of the others may have a unique objective that may or may not accord with those of others.)

"Where" do we want to end up?

"Be very careful. If you don't know where you're going, you might not get there."

Yogi Berra

I find that most games—including those secret games within organizations—are ultimately "about" getting to some "where". Put differently, what really matters in a game is not what you DO, but rather where you want to BE at the end.

In football or soccer, your aim is to "be" across the goal line with the ball. Tennis is "about" getting the ball past your opponent more times that the opponent slips it past you. In golf, the aim is to get the ball into the hole with fewest strokes. In chess, it's to get to the position where you can check the opponent's king.

It's not really about having the perfect golf swing, or the perfect tennis serve: it's ultimately about getting to where you want to be in the end. Having that kind of a clear, measurable goal in mind helps cut through the static, distractions and irrelevancies.

That "where" you want to be at the end may be a real *physical place*, or it may be a *state of mind* ("relieved" "satisfied at a job well done"), or it may be a *situation* in which "everything works well," or "we're now in accord and ready to work together again."

Why *"where you want to be at the end"* rather than *"what you want to accomplish"*? True, in one sense they are much alike, but I find a subtle but important difference. "Accomplish" focuses on the apparent tasks to be done, while "where at the end" brings me more to envisioning what I'm really after, rather than what apparent steps lay ahead. I find I work more effectively with a clear vision of "where at the end," and am better able to cut to the core of it all.

Carry-away point: In the games of career and life, in the end, it's not really not what you want to DO, but rather where you want to BE when it's over.

- With that kind of clear, measurable end in mind, you can then work backward through what it takes to get there. It's like taking a winding route to drive someplace, then, once there, having the sense of the most direct route back.

- An aside from my experience: In some mysterious way, it seems that once I have a desired end clearly in mind, coincidences and synchronicities seem to occur spontaneously, opening channels that smooth the way to that desired outcome. Maybe it's simply that with that end-vision in mind I am more open and alert to opportunities. Maybe it is that. But I'm increasingly convinced there is more to it than random chance . . . as I've explored in my book *Joining Miracles: Navigating the Sea of Synchronicities.*

Here are some questions useful in breaking out that "where" and "when".

1.1   Is this where I ULTIMATELY need to arrive? Or is there something I need even more than that? That is, is this in fact the desired END, or just a MEANS to that end?

"Montie recalls sitting in meetings where Gutierrez [new CEO of Kellogg] would interrupt anyone who dared to give results in pounds of product sold, not in dollars. 'Volume is a means to an end — not an end.' he would say. 'What counts is dollars.' "

From *Fortune* magazine

The point was not so obvious to others who had been locked in on the old measure of success: Now the ultimate test would not be how many pounds of product are delivered to stores, but rather how many dollars are brought to the bank.

Joanna, in the midst of a divorce, is venting to friends about her ex-husband. "I tell you this: I am going to do every possible thing I can to make his life as miserable as possible. Everything."

After a long silence, one of the friends asks, "Are you sure this is what you really want to do with your life? Do you really want to go on churning up the old hurt and anger? Wouldn't you really prefer to move on from this, and live in peace?"

Joanna was focused on what she wanted to DO: to get revenge. The friend's question prodded her to look beyond that to the ultimate outcome: where she wanted TO BE when all was said and done. That is, to be getting on with a new life, unencumbered by anger and revenge.

Nora is filling in for her boss, the project manager, who's on extended sick leave and may not be coming back. That boss' boss is away on assignment, so she finds herself meeting with the Regional Manager, visiting the office for the day.

When the Regional Manager asks how things are going, Nora tells him that her greatest difficulty has been in getting the team to work together.

"How can I help?" he responds.

She goes into more detail on some of the issues, wanting to give him a better sense of the difficulties she has been facing these past few weeks. She's hoping that if she can make him aware of all the details, then he can tell her the best way of handling the situation.

He asks again, "How can I help?"

She vents more, hoping that he will see how hard she's been trying, and hoping, too, that he'll have a solution for her.

After a couple of minutes, the Regional Manager's eyes seem to click shut. A couple of days later, he sends in someone from headquarters to head the project.

Nora's objective was to make the Regional Manager aware of just how tough it was to take over the project so he would understand the challenge. He tried to open her up to the broader possibilities, by asking, "How can I help?" That was another way of asking, "Tell me where you want to be, and what you need from me to enable you to accomplish it?" But, focused too narrowly on the problems, she passed up the opportunity to go beyond.

A story from a very long time ago:

I'm in Ealing, a leafy London suburb, a million or so years ago. It's the first morning of my first independent project as a management consultant. I am there to train the staff of a British consulting firm in a new technology.

I am ushered into the Managing Director's office "to say hello and have a cup of tea." (Nothing seems unusual about that: this is England, after all, and tea is a British tradition.)

Cyril, the Managing Director, has the stuffy manner of an Oxford don . . . which he had in fact been.

But, as I will learn, he had also been an British commando officer.

After the preliminaries, Cyril sits back in his chair, steeples his fingers, peers over the top of the steeple at me, pauses, then says, "Now tell me, what is this project of yours all about?"

The question surprises me. After all, the contract had been negotiated by Con, his second-in-command, who is sitting in on our meeting. I look over at Con, assuming he will handle the question. Con looks back at me, an expectant look on his face.

What the project is about? Of course I'd thought that through, back when I was starting to prepare the training program. I quote what I'd written then. "Upon completion of the training, your people will be able to . . ." And so on.

After a bit, Cyril raises his hand: Stop. "Very good," he says. "You're telling us the training objectives. Very important to plan in advance what our people will learn, of course. But what I'm asking is a somewhat broader version of that question."

I wait, puzzled, while he lights his pipe. Wasn't training the point of this training program?

"What I want to know," Cyril continues, "is what we are ultimately trying to accomplish through this project. It seems to me that your focus is focused solely on the training objectives—what our people will learn."

He lights the pipe again and draws on it before adding, "I accept as a given that our people will have learned all that you say. But now I'm asking you to look beyond to the broader issue: Specifically, how will this project assist our firm in achieving its broader objectives?"

Before I can respond, he adds, "Also, specifically how will we assess—in that larger context—whether it has been successful? How will we measure that success?"

Con finally speaks up. "Your training objectives tell us what our people will learn, and that's important, no question of that. But Cyril is asking you to look beyond that, and put the purpose of the training in context: As you view this, what are we ultimately trying to accomplish through this project? That is, how will we recognize that it has been successful?"

Post-script: I managed to survive that first meeting, and my training program was later used by that firm in training several hundred of their clients in Africa. I was even invited back a couple of years later for another longer consulting project. But that had been a very difficult first hour, fumbling as I was to come up with an answer to a question that for which I had not prepared for.

1.2 On what time-frame am I working: short, mid, or long-term?

- This immediate moment, including the next thing I do or say?

- The course of today, or in the course of my next meeting or phone call?

- This specific project?

- Over the course of the next few months or year?

- The job I now hold?

- The course of my overall career and life?

1.3 Given that time and resources are always finite, why this over all other possibilities?

There's never energy, time, or budget enough to do everything we might like to accomplish . . . or that others are pushing to get done. Inevitably, some goals must be sacrificed.

Beyond that is the issue of "opportunity cost". Whenever you set out to achieve one objective, you do so at the cost of failing to achieve (or even attempt) other potential goals. Therefore, better make sure that what you set out to do is *an end that really matters* —to you, your boss, or your client.

Life is short, but especially short in managerial jobs. You may have only a few months to make your mark before moving on . . . or before becoming vulnerable. It's shorter still if you're a start-up entrepreneur, where "life" may be only as long as your beginning capital permits.

If you're in business, it may seem that the most important objective is to increase sales. But there's usually *an even broader objective: to increase profits, not just sales*. If your focus is too narrow, you could end up adding customers that cost more to service than they add to the bottom line.

If you're an employee, your objective may seem to be to win a certain promotion. But there may be an even broader objective: to enhance your overall career growth. If you look from that broader perspective, you might see that this promotion might turn out to be a career dead-end.

- Is this what I really, ultimately want to accomplish? Why?

- Why this over all other possibilities?

- If not this, then what?

1.4   What elements do I NEED as part of this goal? What elements do I NOT want, or are not essential?

When setting the objective, sometimes it's at least as important to pare away what you don't really need as it is to determine what you *do* need.

The template below is a simple tool for sorting out your insights on the "must-have " factors from those that are only "nice-to-have" or " do not want / need".

Elements that must exist	Nice but not essential	I do not want or need

1.5   Suppose I DO accomplish this, then what?

Trevor pushes hard to have the new marketing initiative brought in his section. He wins. Then he realizes he doesn't have the staff or expertise to handle it. Beyond that, upper management has largely lost interest in this, and is not going to give him what he may need. He's on his own. If it flops, it falls on his back.

Remember the old saying about being careful about what you pray for . . . because you just might get it.

What if you do get what you set out to accomplish, only to realize it brings a new set of complications? So, better ask, early-on, Will achieving this goal yield what I *really* want or need?

- If I do achieve this goal, will that in fact give me what I need?

- If I do succeed, will the present problem situation be resolved in a satisfactory way?

- That is, will it solve the problem that's at the heart of the "game?" Will it bring on new complications?

- Will accomplishing this goal likely turn out to have been worth the cost in factors such as the time and effort expended, time it took to implement, and the like?

- How serious are the risks that achieving (or even just working toward) that objective will bring about unintended consequences, good or bad? (For example, if you undertake this, what are the risks of alienating others, of squandering "political capital," and the like?)

- What are the "opportunity costs" of achieving this objective? That is, what other possible objectives will I have to give up or cut short in order to work toward this?

- What is the *best* thing that can come from achieving this goal?

- What is the *worst* thing likely to come from achieving it (or from investing the time and effort to make the attempt)?

1.6   Is pursuing this really how I want to be spending my energy, creativity, and time? If not, what can I do to change the situation?

We all know people who spend big chunks of their energy—and often their credibility, as well—fighting the system, trying to change the status quo, trying to right what they perceive as wrongs.

The world needs fighters and advocates . . . in *some* cases. They are the folks who bring about change.

But they pay a price — in energy spent, in frustration, in bruised friendships, in the time that could have been used more productively in other ways. You *can* fight City Hall . . . but there's definitely no guarantee that you'll win. Or that it will prove to have been worth the struggle, as well as the ancillary costs to friendships, good-will, and such.

Hence, it's important to recognize from the start that, win or lose, the fight is going to cost time and aggravation. Beyond that, it will distract you from the other things that you could be doing — "opportunity cost."

So, before getting in too deeply, ask questions like these:

- How much is pursuing this going to take out of me personally, and out of my productive hours?

- Suppose I am successful in this: In the end, will it really have been worth the struggle?

- Suppose, when all is finished, not much has really changed. Will I still feel it was worth pursuing this?

- Will I make enemies who may have long memories?

- What else could I be doing with the time, energy and other resources I invest here?

- Which use is likely to be more worthwhile—this use, or pursuing those other ends?

- Which has the best chance of succeeding?

1.7 Check: Is this something that really matters, or am I going for it for trivial reasons, such as to make a report or resume look better?

"Peter's in trouble, but I've seen it coming for a long time. His problem is an insatiable curiosity. He wants to be in on everything, to be copied in on every memo, to attend every meeting. This scatters his energies and cuts into his productive time. As a result, he hasn't got a shelf of products and point to and say, 'There, that's what I've accomplished. That's my track record."

Manager, large tech firm

It's essential to keep in mind that there will never be time or energy enough to do everything well. Before committing precious time and energy to a project, better make sure that an end that really matters to you or your group.

- Ultimately, is this objective (or task) what really matters?

- Is this something that really matters? To me? To the organization?

- Am I just going through the motions, doing what is expected of me or this department?

- Suppose I chose not to pursue this outcome—what then? Would I lose the job? Would Mom disapprove?

- What is the likely worst-case if I do not pursue this? For that matter, *is* there a "worst case"? Is there a chance that what seems worst might turn out to be best?

1.8   If you find it difficult to choose among alternative possible goals, which has ultimate priority? Why?

What if, the more you think about it, you find that you're torn between two apparently incompatible goals? Like choosing whether to vacation at the seashore or the mountains? Or whether to buy a new car or save the money? Or to go into business for yourself, or to minimize risk?

The template below is a tool to help you sort out some of the key factors that often come into conflict in setting goals: possible pay-off, risk, cost, likelihood of success, effect on your relations with other people or departments. Add other factors specific to the unique situation you face.

Factors to consider. Add others specific to your situation.	Goal A	Goal B	Goal C
Which offers the **highest payoff** if I am successful in accomplishing it?			
Which entails the **greatest risk**? **Least risk**?			
Which has the highest costs—both direct and indirect?			
Which in my present judgment, based on what I now know, seems most likely to work out **best in the longer term**?			
Which offers the likelihood of the best and smoothest **relations with other people and departments**?			

Summary

<u>Question 1</u>

How do I (my team) "win"? That is, "Where" do we want or need to be afterward, and how will we recognize that we've arrived there?

1.1   Is this where I ULTIMATELY need to arrive? Or is there something I need even more than that? That is, is this in fact the desired END, or just a MEANS to that end?

1.2   On what time-frame am I working: short, mid, or long-term?

1.3   Given that time and resources are always finite, why this over all other possibilities?

1.4   What elements do I NEED as part of this goal? What elements do I NOT want, or are not essential?

1.5   Suppose I DO accomplish this, then what?

1.6   Is pursuing this really how I want to be spending my energy, creativity, and time? If not, what can I do to change the situation?

1.7   Check: Is this something that really matters, or am I going for it for trivial reasons, such as to make a report or resume look better?

1.8   If you find it difficult to choose among alternative possible goals, which has ultimate priority? Why?

Question 2

Who else is involved in this "game"? What is likely to be their idea of "winning"?

A manager on the headquarters staff of a high-tech firm I worked with in London had the reputation of being "the smartest guy in the company." I asked him about that; here's how he responded:

"That's flattering to hear, but my secret is simple enough: I do my homework.

"What IS my 'homework?' It's making a practice of constantly asking myself 'What if this occurs?' And, 'What if that occurs?' And, 'What if things fail to go according to plan?' And, 'What if there's more going on in this meeting than seems apparent on the surface?'

"At night, when I'm on the way home from work, I replay in my mind one or two key events of the day. I try to break away from the emotions I may have felt at the time, and ask myself what was really going on. As I drive along, I ask "What was really going on? What were we ultimately squabbling over? Was it just today's issue, or were some people positioning themselves for the future? Or were they re-fighting old battles?"

"I look for decision points where the meeting branched one way or the other. I try to figure why it went the way it did. Maybe there's something I can learn from that about how to win people over. Or maybe it was someone calling in chits from past favors.

"I focus on the key players, looking particularly for what I can expect from them in the future. Never mind what they said, what were they really after? Why did they want it? Whose help did they get? What were they willing to trade for that help? Who wanted to stop them from getting it? Why?

"You might ask why I spend my energy doing this? Why don't I just listen to music and forget things? In the first place, it makes life more interesting. I have a curious mind: I want to understand what's really going on.

"But it's also the best training one could possibly get. Every day is like analyzing a business school case study. Things do fall into patterns. By having thought through what really went on today, I'll be better prepared for what comes up next time, and I'll have thought out a range of responses I can make then."

2.1   Who are the other "players"—directly or indirectly? Why? What is their involvement?

First issue, just who *are* the other "players" in this game?

You might assume, because you and your managers and peers all work for the same company or the same government agency, that you are all playing on the same team, with the same objective—to make the company profitable, or to make the agency effective . . . or at least to keep the employer up and running, and their jobs carrying on smoothly.

But if you burrow down into what's really happening within the company or agency, you'll typically find that there are often about as many "sides" within an organization game as there are people or departments . . . with each playing the game to their own benefit.

Joe wants to keep the company in business so his job continues. But he also wants to win a promotion, and he may think that means he needs to make himself appear outstanding . . . even if that means holding back some information or cooperation that would help Dana in the next office, because Dana might be competing for the same promotion.

The Manager of Division A (or Bureaucracy A) might have a policy of hoarding information—given the mind-set of knowledge is power. If Division B is unaware of that important info, then Manager A can one-up Manager B, and thereby (so he assumes) make himself look smarter than B . . . which will (again so he assumes) translate to a bigger budget, more jobs slots, and ultimately a promotion.

Granted, they may be playing for *personally* unselfish ends—that is, may believe they are doing it for the good of the company, not just for their own personal good, or the good of their department. But their perception of the proper objective may be shaped by their role, or in what office they work.

In other words, they're all (nominally) on the same team . . . but they're each playing different games, with different perceptions of what winning means.

"Virtual" players in the game

Sometimes the real players aren't even visible on the game field: they may be in the background, trying to get their goals accomplished through others . . . without revealing their own interest, and without taking any political risks.

Checklist: Spotting who else may have an interest in this, and why

The checklist here will get you started. Add other items from your experience.

- Who are the key people, such as the ultimate decision makers, or the *influencers* of an upcoming decision?

- In spotting who else may be players in this game, ask, Who stands to gain if this works (or if it fails)? Who stands to lose? ("Who" may include individuals, departments, or other kinds of groups.)

- What does each want? That is, What will it take for them to emerge from this situation feeling that they have succeeded? How does each win? How might each lose?

- Whose advice, "buy-in," or support (financial, organizational clout, "political" etc.) do I need?

- Who are (supposedly) my "allies?' Why—friendship? job title? mutual interest? What do they want? Are the interests of these allies—at least for this one project—identical with mine? If not, how do we differ?

- Who are my probable adversaries? Why? What do they want?

- Are there "hidden players," such as players operating through others, or manipulating other people? What do they want?

- What other agendas might be operating?

- Who benefits if things go well? If things go poorly?

- Of these other people, what are they rewarded for, or punished for, in this matter? Therefore, what pressures are they responding to?

2.2   How does each of these "players" win? That is, what problem are they likely trying to solve, and how will they measure success?

The rules of tennis and chess and golf and bridge are clear, and every player knows what those rules are.

But the rules of the games that go on within organizations are often kept secret.

First of all, the game—and the real rules—tend to be constantly shifting.

Beyond that, it's to the advantage of the players to keep even the *existence* of the game secret, let alone to reveal what it is they are really after. (Still another instance of how knowledge is power.)

The Romans had a saying, *Cui bono?* which translates as "Who benefits?" The point is, if you can look through the surface appearances to find who gains if a situation goes a certain way, then you gain valuable insight into what is really going on in that situation, as well as who are the most interested players.

The same advice, this time in a different language: "If you have trouble understanding what's really going on in a situation, follow the trail of the dollars. Find who gets what share of the rewards, for doing what. Once you know where the money goes, the puzzle will begin untangling itself.

Then to figure what each is after. To do that, ask, for each player,

- Suppose I were that person (or the department or other constituency they represent), What would I be trying to accomplish here?

- If I were that person, how would I recognize whether I have been successful?

Checklist: Some common "wins"

Authority.

- Who will be in charge? Who presently is in control? Is this being tested?

Bear in mind that where the real authority rests may be very different from what the formal organization chart indicates. Often, the real power rests with the person strong enough to claim and use it. Or the assistant to the top executive may be the real power, because that's the person who does most of the work and in reality makes most of the decisions, with the nominal head only a figurehead who signs off on whatever is put before him.

Direction.

- Whose objectives are going to be given priority? Whose methods will be used in achieving these objectives?

Resources.

- Who gets what share of the budget? Which department gets extra equipment, space, personnel?

Rewards.

- Who gets rewards and raises? Who gets extra "perks" such as better offices and assignments?

"Turf."

- Here we're referring to turf in the broader sense not only of physical space, but also of freedom to set directions and priorities without being impinged upon by others.

Ultimate "win."

- If nothing else, holding onto the job and not getting fired, demoted, or sent to the organization's Siberia may be considered a win.

The template below is a tool for sorting out these issues.

Who else? Direct? Indirect?	Likely allies? Interests align with ours?	Likely opponents? Interests compete with ours?	For each: what does "winning" mean?	Other considerations?

2.3 What are the other "players" rewarded for, or punished for? What implications result?

As you work with people over a span of time, you tend to develop a sense of their personalities, and of the factors that induce them to act as they do.

But personality is only one of several factors that contribute to the behaviors you encounter.

But look beyond the formalities of their job. Look for where the individuals are positioned in the organization's hierarchy. What responsibilities flow from the job they hold?

Who do they report to? "Who" both in the sense of job title, but also regarding the personality factors and motivations of the person in that higher-level job. What "hat" the individual is wearing in this present role may dictate how they look at things. If their boss is a demanding nit-picker, then very likely they will be one as well . . . for self-preservation.

Look also for the subtle rewards and punishments they encounter. For example, are they more likely to be rewarded for doing something innovative? Or are they more likely to be punished in some way for making mistakes? How do the rewards for being innovative or going the extra mile, balance out against the punishments that may come for making a mistake or stepping over some invisible line?

How would these factors impact on the way they react to new ideas you bring to them, perhaps for cutting costs, or improving the quality of your section's output? Some considerations:

- What *pressures* are they feeling? What implications for me and the way I relate to them?

- Who are the *key judges* of their performance? What criteria do those judges likely use? (On this issue of Who the important judges are, see Question 5.4.)

- What *rewards* are they seeking? What punishments are they avoiding?

- Are they still energetic and ambitious? Or has the system worn them down? What are the *implications* for how you work with them?

Summary

Question 2

Who else is involved in this "game"? What is likely to be their idea of "winning"?

2.1   Who are the other "players"—directly or indirectly? Why? What is their involvement?

2.2   How does each of these "players" win? That is, what problem are they likely trying to solve, and how will they measure success?

2.3   What are the other "players" rewarded for, or punished for? What implications result?

Question 3

What's really going on here? Is this a real issue, or a subtle test?

"On my first morning in the new job, the branch manager asked me to come into his office and bring my steno pad. Then he dictated for hours without stopping. Noon came and went, and then one o'clock passed.

"Finally I said, 'What about lunch?' His reply was, 'Oh, is it that time already?'

"Later, one of the people who had been there a while told me this was a game he tried with everyone, to see how far he could push. If you let him get away with it, then you lost his respect, and that showed up in other ways."

Secretary, federal agency

That secretary was my mother, way back when. There are no steno pads these days, but the lesson stuck with me.

The tests and probes usually begin on small matters that seem too minor to warrant making an issue. But if you let them pass, then the pattern has been set.

Sometimes the person doing the testing may not even consciously *intend* a test—at least not at the start. They might begin by pushing the limits just a little, sometimes without really intending to. If they find there are no consequences, they might push a little more, then still more.

They might come in late one day. Next week, a couple of times. If no one seems to notice or care, arriving late becomes the norm.

Or the co-worker who's sharing your office begins to spread things out. You say nothing at first. Maybe you don't even notice. Or it doesn't seem worth making a fuss about. Before long, you're down to one quarter of a two-person office. A precedent has been set, and that person and others will expect you to follow the same pattern.

If you wait too long to re-establish boundaries, then you may very well face the claim of unfairness: "You didn't mind the last time, so why now?" Or, "You let Allison do that, why not me?"

- Stay alert. Be polite . . . but wary. Maybe this is *not* just a random happening.

- Be open and direct in preserving your rights or your turf. If you have been assigned half an office, you have every right to all of your half.

- Be as subtle in protecting your turf as the other person has been in invading it. Probes are subtle, both to test you and to allow "deniability," so the prober can back off with a muttered apology and no loss of face. If you react too directly to a subtle probe, then you'll appear to have overreacted to a minor issue. You'll lose face and weaken yourself for the future.

3.1   Is this really *just* a coincidence? Or is it a subtle test?

When you take a course in defensive driving, you're taught to run through in your mind the various What-if scenarios that may arise on the road.

The point is to train you to develop a kind of "rational paranoia," an alertness that there could be hidden dangers ahead.

Survival in organizations requires a mindset a lot like defensive driving, remaining constantly aware that other people don't always do the right things, and aren't always rational. Sometimes they really *are* out to get you, and you have to be ready for the unpredictable.

"Sometimes even paranoids have real enemies."

Henry Kissinger

You're not the only person who wants—or wants to *keep*—a really good job.

Your competition may try to compete only on capabilities, skills, resumes and references. Then again, they may also play some subtle ploys to throw you off stride.

Similarly, the "gate-keepers" to those better jobs are likely to test the candidates in some non-obvious ways. One of the unspoken rules of the game is that you need to be constantly alert and tuned in. Even when it seems you've made it safely, there may still be surprises to come:

"It was supposed to be the final interview for a sales job. The boss appeared, well-dressed as always—Brooks Brothers suit, Gucci shoes, a necktie that probably cost as much as my first car. But his fly was open.

"Should I tell him? Will he be offended? I decided to mention it.

"He laughed. 'Okay, Alan, you've got the job. That was a test. I couldn't hire anybody who didn't have the guts to tell me something to my face.'"

Alan Graham

3.2 Are they trying to manipulate me? What are they really after?

Manipulation echoes what Andy Warhol said of art: It's "whatever you can get away with."

We can usually recognize when manipulation takes the form of sudden, phony friendliness and solicitude.

But the opposite—what seems to be dislike or condescension—may be a different kind of manipulative ploy.

Maybe the other person is hoping to bully you on this matter, or to intimidate you so that you back off, either now or next time.

Or maybe they're expecting that their phony hostility will throw you off-stride, causing you to be more conciliatory, less inclined to confront them or to take risks.

Or they may guess that you will react to their subtle signals by pushing back in a visible way at a time when others see only that one side of the interchange; making you appear to be "difficult," even irrational.

Checklist: Common manipulation techniques

- Are they trying to get at me by playing on my fears and insecurities?

- Is there a hook in the compliment they're paying? Do they really appreciate what I've done, or are they just setting me up, hence leading me on by telling me what they think I want to hear?

- Are there subtle incongruities, such as brief flashes of impatience showing through the "niceness"? Is this person basically the same when "on-stage" and off?

- How do they operate with other people when they don't know I'm watching?

- Suppose they are offering to do a favor for me now, maybe something I have not asked for. But what if I were to ask for a *different* small favor—would they be likely to agree at once, without working out how they can use it to their benefit?

- Overall, what are my intuitions telling me right now? Does this feel "off"— maybe too good to be true?

3.3   Is this a dominance test? Is it a "red-flag" test?

"Practice losing your temper in a controlled way. Let everyone know that you have a threshold, that you are prone to blowing up.

"But when you lose your temper, don't really lose it. Keep it controlled and focused. That gives you authority, and it puts you in a leadership role. It lets you control the situation."

Government executive, former Army colonel

Maybe that crazy boss, or the seemingly crazy client with the hair-trigger temper, aren't really crazy, after all. Maybe they've learned to use sudden, unexpected flare-ups as a tool to shock people, intentionally throwing them off-balance so they try even harder to please.

Unless you're attuned to the trick, you may even find yourself apologizing, thereby setting yourself up to later grant them some special favor to "make up" for precipitating this incident. If you do that, they'll be back for more later, and again, and again.

Here are some other kinds of tests and ploys to be alert for:

Subtle encroachments on your turf

Over a period of several weeks, another manager "borrows" one of your people to help out on a series of what he terms "special projects".

Gradually, these projects slip in as part of your person's normal routine. Before you realize what has happened, much of their time is spent doing the work of the other department, and you have in effect been manipulated out of part of your staff.

"Red flag" issues

The matador waves the red flag to enrage the bull (at least so goes the legend). But Red Flags can also work as manipulation tools with humans, as well.

Example: Suppose you are making a presentation, and one of the attendees begins nitpicking a series of minor issues. Or questions your methodology or experience. Beware: they may be waving these as Red Flags to distract you, and hence to defuse the power of your presentation.

If you rise to the bait and defend on each of these probes, you fritter away time and energy, and will likely lose the impetus of the presentation. (Which may be exactly what the nitpicker wanted: To stop your idea, or maybe just to deflect your argument, or your train of thought.)

Beyond that, if you take these minor issues seriously enough to respond to, they may then assume disproportionate importance in the eyes of the others.

How *should* you deal with distractions like these? One option is to acknowledge them as *suggestions* to be considered, then move on without letting the discussion bog down on details.

Or you could respond to the effect, "You're right, I did overlook that. I'll make a note and deal with it later. But now let's move on." By "accepting" their comment or suggestion, you demonstrate that you respect for their input, though you are not necessarily agreeing to make the changes. That kind of response may defuse the issue.

Intrusion into your body space

We Americans tend to keep a ring of "personal space" around us, usually at least three feet—roughly arms' length—in the front, and we become uncomfortable if anyone other than family or close friends enter that space.

That expectation gives "manipulatives" a tool to work with. They may deliberately move in towards you much closer than normal, intentionally violating that expected ring of personal space. What happens? The victim will—on a subliminal level—feel crowded and even dominated. They may back away, further projecting defensiveness. In any case, that pressure may cause them to lose focus on the issue at hand, get rattled, and give way just to get more space.

> *The story goes that Lyndon Johnson, when he was a leader in the Senate, was notorious for grabbing a fellow senator in a "friendly" bear-hug, holding him close, spittle flying, while persuading him to vote the LBJ way. Not many held out for long.*

In short, what seems an accidental intrusion into your personal space may be an intentional distraction as well as a subtle test of your personal strength and confidence. If you "back off" in this subliminal confrontation, they expect that you will be inclined to back off in a "real" confrontation.

Heavy intentional silences

Intrusion into our personal space makes us uncomfortable.

So does silence—particularly when it comes suddenly in the middle of a conversation or discussion.

See for yourself: Test the power of silence. Not with a close friend, because good friends can tolerate silences. But see what happens with an acquaintance or somebody from work. Just stop talking, and notice how quickly they begin to show visible discomfort with the silence. (True, you will also probably feel the pressure of this silence, but you know what's happening.)

Skilled police interrogators and astute sales people use the power of silence to their advantage, knowing the other person will feel pressured to fill that silence.

> *"Hack Ames was good at his job. He had all the tricks. . . . A good questioner will ask a question, get what sounds like a complete answer and sit there in silence, mildly quizzical, until you qualify or add to the answer. A good questioner will ask very simple questions requiring short and simple answers and slowly increase the pace until when he throws a curve, the silence seems to last too long, and you feel a compulsion to give an answer quickly. Any answer."*

> John D. MacDonald. *The Empty Copper Sea*

> *"Epstein sat back a little and sipped some coffee. He was in no hurry. He was never in any hurry. He had all the time he needed. He'd get to where he was going when he needed to. I was getting tired of waiting for him. Which I knew was also a tactic. What would I say to get him talking. When in doubt, go with what you do best. I shut up."*

> Robert B. Parker, *Cold Service*

Subtle verbal techniques

The other person might intentionally (but subliminally) project the assumption that you will—naturally! of course!—go along with what they are suggesting.

Watch for phrases like, "*When* you . . ." instead of "*If* you . . ." ("If you" leaves open that you have a choice, while "when you" subtly closes your door, implying the decision is settled.)

Watch also for time-lines and deadlines being put forward "for approval" when the basic issue of whether or not to actually proceed hasn't yet been decided. "If you" leaves open that you have a choice, while "when you" subtly closes your door, implying the decision is settled.

Projected dislike or lack of respect

Police are not the only ones who use this method. Non-verbal signals of apparent personal dislike or hostility may actually be subtle tests to see how far you can be pushed.

Or they may be coded messages.

> "When our budget was cut back, my boss told me that I could have as much time as I needed to find a new job. But then he started freezing me out in subtle ways, like not telling me of meetings I should be attending, or keeping information from me. Most of all, he became personally very aloof, even cold, when talking with me. For example, I pulled off a real coup for him in salvaging part of the operation, and he didn't say a word of thanks, whereas before he'd have gone out of his way to flatter me.

> "During this period, he had me come every few days to his other office, which was at the university. The way he had the office arranged there, the desk lamp was pointed so it glared in my eyes. Because I'd seen him operate so much before, I was sure that he was aware of what he was doing, and that he was using the lamp as a tactic to help him maintain control. I guess he wanted to make me uncomfortable and ill-at-ease so I would sub-consciously feel unwelcome and quit sooner.

> "My suspicion was confirmed the day something came up suddenly and he realized he needed me to stay on a couple of extra months. Again he brought me into the office, and the

lamp was in my eyes for the first part of the meeting, while he tended to some administrative matters. But then as the topic switched and we got into the area in which he needed something from me, he suddenly became very concerned with my comfort. At that point in the conversation, he turned the light off and changed his manner and became the old 'warm uncle' again while he talked about how valuable I was and whether possibly I could extend my time there."

Former administrative manager, Washington think tank

3.4   What's really going on in this meeting?

We wrap up this section on looking through to what's really going on by taking a look at the ultimate game-field—meetings. Meetings are a petri dish for subtle games and gamesmanship, and you sit in them sit there and watch stuff grow and evolve. (For much the same reason, meetings are ideal learning laboratories.)

It's usually in meetings that the players push for the resources they need, and push also for recognition and psychological victories.

In meetings, too, players may be trying to knock others out of the game.

Here's a checklist to help you develop perspective on what may otherwise be too familiar.

Checklist: Looking through the surface of meetings
The attendees and their goals

- Who is present at this meeting? Why? How do they "win?" That is, from their perspective, how will they recognize that it has been a successful meeting? What is the best thing, and worst thing, that could flow from this meeting?

- Who is NOT present? Why not? Were they not invited? Is that a clue that they are "cut out of the loop?" Or did they choose not to attend so they could later claim they played no part in what they expect will be unsuccessful?

- For each attendee (or department represented at the meeting): is there something specific they be likely to want from this meeting, or are they merely "sitting in"

- What "power clusters" are evident? Who is teaming up? With whom? Against whom?

- What overt "constituencies" are represented, such as an attendee who is representing a department?

- What covert or hidden players are acting through those who are present? Who are the "puppets?" Who is pulling their strings? Are the puppets aware that they are being used? If so, what do they want? What do those who are pulling the puppets' strings hoping to achieve?

Control

- Who is nominally in control of this meeting? Is that the senior person present? Is it the person who called the meeting? If not, why not?

- Is someone questing to take over—perhaps in subtle ways such as blocking movement, raising distractions, trying to dominate the discussion, trying to shift the agenda, and the like?

Status signals

- What signals are sent by factors such as where the attendees sit, who is positioned close to the meeting leader, how the leader reacts to the various attendees' contributions, how the others react to comments?

- What are the tones of the communications? Do those tones vary depending on who is speaking? Friendly? Brusque? Dismissive? Interrupted? Ignored?

- What happens to the ideas put forward by the various attendees? Whose inputs are accepted with respect, at least to the point of being rationally discussed? Whose inputs are immediately attacked? Whose are ignored? Why is this happening?

- What IS being said? What is NOT being said: Are the attendees ignoring the proverbial elephant in the room? Why?

Effectiveness / conclusions reached

- Does the meeting end with actual progress having been made? Have specific, concrete action steps been agreed upon?

- If not, why not? Was the leader ineffective? Or did power clusters block progress?

- Overall, who "won?" Who lost?

Summary

Question 3

What's really going on here? Is this a real issue, or a subtle test?

3.1   Is this really *just* a coincidence? Or is it a subtle test?

3.2   Are they trying to manipulate me? What are they really after?

3.3   Is this a dominance test? Is it a "red-flag" test?

3.4   What's really going on in this meeting?

Question 4

What is this situation ultimately about? Where is the "crunch"?

It's helpful to view games, especially within organizations, as ultimately about solving problems. In games at work, the various players usually have differing perceptions of the core of the problem, and usually measure success (or victory) differently.

In a well-managed organization, there will never be enough resources to fill every possibility—that is, resources like budget increases, extra staff, best offices, raises and promotions.

The fact is, it's usually a *good* thing that there's not quite enough to fill every worthwhile need, as organizations that operate lean usually operate best. The competition for resources brings out creativity, along with higher levels of energy and focus.

Most of the "games" at work are about genuine competition or conflict for resources from people with different ideas, responsibilities, and perspectives. These games and competitions tend to be generally beneficial, at least in the longer term. That competition provides a useful internal form of checks and balances. Ideally, most of those competitions will benefit the organization, as people compete by coming up with the best ideas and the highest productivity.

But not always. Organizations are made up of people, and people are only human (for better or worse!), and hence some conflicts and competitions are about ego, empire-building, defensiveness, and downright orneriness, vindictiveness, and power-hunger.

These games may devolve one of two forms: Either a Zero-sum game (for me to win, you must lose), or a Positive-sum game (we all work together so 1+1 becomes 3, or even 5).

Ideally, all will be playing with the Positive-sum mindset. But that's not always the case, and the Zero-sum folks are not likely to say otherwise and give up their advantage.

In this chapter, we'll be examining some questions helpful in looking through situations in order to spot the real core of the conflicts in which you may find yourself enmeshed . . . whether as observer or participant.

4.1   Is this a real conflict over real things? Or is it just a matter of some personalities getting crosswise with each other?

Another way of putting it: "Am I (or the other party) being strong, or just being a pain?"

"Roy is an aggressive, competent guy. Let me be clear on that. To say that a manager is 'aggressive' is usually a positive statement, as it means that they step forward to deal with challenges, instead of sitting back hiding from them. It implies they are 'pro-active,' instead of 're-active.' It means they have confidence and have no fear of competing to see whose ideas and approaches are better. That's all good.

"But Roy can't keep his aggressiveness and competitiveness under control. He's compulsively competitive. It's not only when he's going for a promotion—competitiveness in that context I can understand. But play handball with him, and he'll break his neck—or yours—to win. He just can't seem to discriminate the occasions in which it's important to win from those when it's not.

"He's the same in meetings. He can't stand to lose on any point, no matter how minor, and he'll push so damned hard for his ideas that he turns everybody off, including the boss.

"The bottom line is that he's the classic case of the guy so obsessive about winning every skirmish that he can't see it's causing him to lose the war."

Corporate manager, speaking of a peer

"You need to be diplomatically aggressive here. I mean being aggressive as hell, yet still being diplomatic. A lot of people can be aggressive. The great ones can be aggressive ten times a day without making any enemies."

Government Executive, Ph.D. scientist, former Army colonel

A tool to pinpoint the core of the (possible) conflict

The template below is a tool for cutting to the heart of what the conflict is actually about.

The example shows how it would work if we were trying to get a handle on an impending conflict with Roy (the compulsively competitive guy in the quotation above)

For the example, we'll assume that Roy and I are peer team managers; Roy heads one team, and I head the other.

I want:	Roy likely wants:
To get two new-hires on my team to help with our increased workload.	Even though my team has a need for people that Roy's does not, he makes it clear that for us to add bodies would be "unfair". He will want to make the case for splitting them, one for each team.
Why it matters to me:	**Why it matters to Roy:**
Our workload has escalated, and must get done on-time; otherwise we may lose customers.	Roy tends to see everything as a Zero-sum power game: that is, he loses face if he does not gain staff. He will likely feel personally diminished and his position threatened if he does not come away with something from this.

Try it. Focus on some situation, present or past, in which what should have been a simple, straight-forward interaction turned surprisingly difficult. Use the template as a tool to find what real differences in objectives exist between the parties, and why those differing objectives likely matters to them.

Are multiple groups involved? Then you can extend the template, like this:

I want:	Opponent A likely wants:	Opponent B likely wants:
Why it matters to me:	**Why it matters to A:**	**Why it matters to B:**

4.2 Is this conflict (or looming conflict) really about the present situation, or is it about something from the past or future?

You're in a new job, attending your first staff meeting. Suddenly, you find yourself caught in a nasty squabble over what seems to be a minor issue.

Is this just a case of somebody picking on you because they don't like your looks?

Or have you walked into the middle of the latest skirmish in an ongoing battle?

Or is somebody picking a fight with you for no other reason than the fact that you're new here, and they're testing your reflexes and smarts?

> *"You're the new kid in town, and the other lawyers are going to be watching to see if you try to compromise on every case. Sooner or later, you're going to have to establish your credibility by taking a case and fighting it to the bitter end. Show them that you are willing to go to trial, that you are willing to scrap over every point along the way.*
>
> *"Once you establish the fact that you will fight when necessary, then you'll find that they are a lot more reasonable about compromising. You can bet that they don't want to take every case to trial any more than you do, but they will test to see whether you have a backbone."*
>
> Advice from Louis Meconi, Esq. when I finished law school

Another instance: a co-worker asks a favor. It's more than you feel comfortable in granting. You turn him down, apologizing as you do.

A few days later, he comes back asking another favor, one that also stretches you more than you'd like. But now you feel you owe him one, and hence feel obliged to grant this favor.

Later, you realize that he deliberately set you up with the first request: he didn't really care about that one, but wanted to be positioned to get the one that mattered

Some considerations:

- Is today's squabble, when you really come down to it, ultimately an attempt to re-fight some issues from the past? What issues? Why?

- Are the parties positioning themselves for the future? What might that be?

- Is one of the parties "borrowing trouble" from the future? That is, being preemptively difficult now, perhaps to set up a bargaining ploy for later?

- Is someone reopening a battle from the past, either for the sake of vengeance, or just to be ornery?

- Is someone feeling terminally frustrated, or maybe threatened? (Even though it makes no rational sense, maybe they are simply acting out . . . or lashing out.)

- Is this squabble a symbolic battle over an altogether different issue altogether? (For instance, a conflict that is ostensibly about a report being delivered late may really be about who gets to control a department, or control the flow of information.)

- Is someone pushing or testing me? Or are they trying to test the system?

Summary

Question 4

What is this situation ultimately about? Where is the "crunch"?

4.1   Is this a real conflict over real things? Or is it just a matter of some personalities getting crosswise with each other?

4.2   Is this conflict (or looming conflict) really about the present situation, or is it about something from the past or future?

Part two:
HOW AM I DOING SO FAR?

In Part One, the focus was on cutting to the core of what game (or games) were being played.

We determined that by looking at these questions in the first group:

<u>Question 1</u> How do *we* "win"? That is, "Where" do we want or need to be afterward, and how will we recognize that we've arrived there?

<u>Question 2</u> Who else is involved in this "game"? What is likely to be their idea of winning?

<u>Question 3</u> What's really going on here? Is this a real issue, or a subtle test?

<u>Question 4</u> What is this situation ultimately about? Where is the crunch?

Now in Part Two, we focus on a different perspective: *In this game, how am I doing so far?*

<u>Question 5</u> Am I being given the recognition and compensation that I *honestly* deserve? If not, why not?

<u>Question 6</u> Am I attuned to the "real rules" that operate here? Is "disinformation" part of the way of life?

<u>Question 7</u> Am I focusing my time and efforts on the ends that matter most?

<u>Question 8</u> Am I learning from the right role models?

<u>Question 9</u> Am I engineering the conditions that lead to success? Or am I setting up for failure?

<u>Question 10</u> Am I willing to trade my comfortable set of self-fulfilling expectations of limited success for more productive expectations that force me to risk and grow?

Question 5

Am I being given the recognition and compensation that I *honestly* deserve? If not, why not?

Ever get the sense that you're not getting the kind of recognition that your talents and efforts deserve—pay and bonuses and promotions, perks, and appreciation? If yes—*honestly* yes—then consider questions like those that follow here.

5.1 Where do the significant dollars go in my organization, profession, or trade? To whom or to what group? Why there?

and

5.2 Is another person (or another department, etc.) getting the rewards, promotions, budget, etc. that should go to me? Who? Why? What can I do?

Money talks, and tends to speak more honestly than words. By tracing where the budget dollars go within your organization, you gain a realistic insight on what is really *valued* there.

By making the effort to assess what kinds of capabilities attract the best assignments, promotions, and bonuses, you gain a clear vision of the real priorities within that organization, and what it considers most vital—in the collective wisdom of the staff as a whole, or in the views of the people who set the rules and rewards.

Compare your department and your job against other people and departments who seem to get the biggest budgets and best rewards. As you do, keep questions like these: in mind:

- What does that comparison tell you about how your section, and your job, are really valued?

- Do promotions come as quickly in your section or area as in other fields or departments?

- How do the career ladders compare — in terms of how fast and how far one can progress?

What if my section comes out short?

Your answers to the three questions above may indicate that your section is in fact not very important — or not *perceived* as important. You may be working in a career backwater, one of those sections that lack pizzazz, and are kept running only because of bureaucratic inertia, or because it's always been there.

Another possibility: even though your unit or job is *important*, it's *not valued* by those who run the place.

In some organizations, for example, those in the administrative sections are looked down upon—or taken for granted. ("It doesn't take a lot of smarts to keep paperwork flowing," the leadership might feel.) Yet in other organizations, it's often the admin types who rule—and tend to take care of themselves first. (Ever work in a university? Or a school district? Then you know what I mean.)

By the same token, a recent article pointed out that engineers fresh out of school start with good pay, but then find their pay stagnating as more and more of the employers' money goes to reward people in sales.

What if my section is in fact a dead-end?

What if you conclude that your job, or the department in which you work, are considered, by the key people, as dead ends?

Option #1: You could develop a public-relations campaign to "educate" your boss and boss' bosses on the value of your contribution.

Maybe. But it may already be too late: once the handwriting is on the wall, it's usually impossible to erase. If you've been tagged as a certain type—of the low-pay, under-appreciated caste—then it may be best to consider going to . . .

Option #2: Pull the plug here ASAP, and start over someplace else.

5.3 If I am not getting the recognition and pay that my work— honestly— deserves, why not?

If not, then why not? Are you just not "visible" enough? Or is there a deeper reason? Are you being sent an unspoken message?

Here are some issues to consider as you explore possible reasons that you may not be getting the recognition you deserve.

- Is what I'm doing, or the way I'm doing it, in fact not particularly valuable to the organization?

- Even if it is valuable, is it not *perceived* as valuable in the eyes of those who dispense rewards—that is, the *important judges*? Is there a way I can either increase the value I provide, or "educate" these judges?

- Have I failed to carve out a niche, making it clear that I add unique value? Is this enough to overcome any belief that others could supply it just as well, or at lower cost?

- Is someone else (or some other department) getting the rewards that should go to me: who? Why? Am I in a backwater department or field to which dollars and recognition do not readily flow?

- Check: Am I perhaps in the wrong career or wrong role? Am I in a job for which there is no strong market need, or for which society or the marketplace does not assign a high value?

- Overall, is there some unstated reason why I am not getting what I deserve? Am I missing some signals? What can I do?

5.4 Who are the important judges? How do they view me and my work? What implications?

Way, way back, only one judge really mattered: the teacher who graded your schoolwork.

But it's not that simple now. Perhaps your supervisor does give out grades, in one form or another—maybe feedback, maybe ranking, or performance reviews. But the supervisor is *usually not the only judge . . . and often not even the most important.*

Other potential key judges

Who those other key judges are will depend on the circumstances and the organization within which you work, but here are some general considerations to get you started.

The boss, and boss' boss.

If you work within an organization, normally your immediate supervisor will be the key judge, and those further up the organizational hierarchy will also be significant

Co-workers.

Your co-workers may also be important judges, as their judgment of you will reflect in how much cooperation and respect they provide.

Customers or clients.

If you're in contact with the ultimate paying customer, then of course that customer matters. But even if your work output goes only to some other department within the agency, that user, your customer, is important, as their satisfaction, or the lack of it, will reflect back.

Self-employed?

If you're self-employed, then your customers or clients will normally be the most important judges. But your peers may also be crucial judges, both for the degree of cooperation they give you, as well as for the referrals they may pass on.

Checklist: Spotting the important judges

- Who are the important judges of how well I'm doing my job? Why are they the key judges, and not others?

- What criteria are they using to judge me and my contribution?

- Are these the most appropriate measures? If not, what *should* be the criteria be, and how can I "educate" them to recognize and judge by the criteria that are truly important?

- Are the *apparent* judges the *truly important* judges? For instance, is my outside client a more important judge than my supervisor? If not, what should I do about it?

- If I am locked in with inappropriate judges, is there a way to bypass them and get the attention of ones who are more appropriate—or more open to me?

- Overall, what are the practical implications for me?

This template serves as a tool for organizing your findings.

Typical key judges	What criteria matter most to them.	Implications.
Manager/supervisor		
Co-workers		
Customers/clients		
Ultimate users		
Shareholders		
Others		

Summary

Question 5

Am I being given the recognition and compensation that I *honestly* deserve? If not, why not?

5.1   Where do the significant dollars go in my organization, profession, or trade? To whom or to what group? Why there?

5.2   Is another person (or another department, etc.) getting the rewards, promotions, budget, etc. that should go to me? Who? Why? What can I do?

5.3   If I am not getting the recognition and pay that my work—honestly—deserves, why not?

5.4   Who are the important judges? How do they view me and my work? What implications?

Question 6

Am I attuned to the "real rules" that operate here? Is "disinformation" part of the way of life?

"Take a look around the office between six and seven in the evening. You'll find a lot of people visible in their offices then, all of them seeming to be churning out reams of work.

"But in the daytime, during normal working hours, chances are you'll find these same people wandering the halls, wasting time in pointless meetings, taking long lunches.

"That's the way the game is played here: you're judged by your visibility in the evening, because that's supposed to show dedication to the company."

Mid-level Manager, technology firm

Organizations and professions usually have some explicit rules— you'll find them in the employee handbook, or somebody will brief you on them your first day on the job.

But if you keep your eyes open and look beneath the platitudes and surface appearances, you'll often find *another set of rules operating—rules that are not in writing, in fact that usually are typically never put into words.* Why the secrecy? Because knowledge is power. The people who know these hidden rules may choose not to pass them on because that knowledge gives them the advantage.

These "Real Rules" sometimes serve as a subtle screening process. Your ability to discover and operate by these hidden criteria tells others whether you have the perceptiveness and flexibility to fit in with the local *cognoscenti*.

"They stress here how important it is for managers to help their people develop to their full potential, how managers should be very concerned with developing a congenial working atmosphere.

"But what's really rewarded for is the ability to exploit resources, including—especially—your people. If you're too people-oriented, if you have too much empathy, you won't make it here. Helping your people takes too long, and here what really matters is getting quick results. They say one thing, but really mean for you to go for the short-term results."

Mid-level manager, major financial institution

You may not *like* or *approve* of the Real Rules that operate in your organization or profession, but it's essential to learn them. Then, if you choose not to abide by them, then that is a sign of independence, not of ignorance.

Some points to keep in mind:

First, these "Real Rules" may change over time, or as conditions change.

Beyond that, the relevant Real Rules may also change as you shift roles within the organization. What is appropriate for you as a junior manager may not be appropriate as you move upward. A model junior manager may be expected to be "hard-charging" and "energetic," while the Rules in the same organization call for senior people to project calmness, confidence, and control. If you remain hard-charging, then you're seen as "insecure," or "overly-aggressive."

Case study: Culture clash of Red v. Blue v. New

In a recent article on Dave Cote, now CEO of Honeywell, *Fortune* said this, and I think the issue is typical of a lot of large organizations (and even some small ones, as well!):

> *"For Cote, job one at Honeywell was halting a raging clash of cultures. Employees called it the "red" and "blue" wars, taken from the traditional logo of the two companies. Red represented the old Honeywell. Its folks were courtly and prided themselves on pleasing the customer. But in practice that meant promising the customers anything, then, say, infuriating aircraft manufacturers by delivering avionics equipment way behind schedule. Blue stood for the former AlliedSignal. Its ethos was in-your-face confrontation, with an emphasis on 'making the numbers' at all costs.*
>
> *To make matters worse, a third wayward culture needed taming. Around the time of the merger, Honeywell absorbed a maker of fire and safety systems named Pittway. Its managers were staunchly independent folks who'd started their own businesses and considered the red and blue factions too incompetent to give them orders."*

In spotting the Real Rules that operate in your organization or profession, look through to the deeper reality by asking questions such as these:

6.1 What are the professed "articles of faith" here? Does the reality differ?

Organizations *do* have cultures, expectations, and items of shared belief.

But organizations (and the movers and shakers that control them) often speak with forked tongues, professing one set of expectations, while really meaning another.

It's risky to take the supposed shared beliefs on faith, without comparing them with the "realities" that actually operate. For example:

The "articles of faith" might proclaim:	While the reality may be:
Your role is clearly defined by the job descriptions and position on the organization chart.	The job description defines the **minimum** you must do. But if you want to get favorably noticed, it's essential to push out and make your output more valuable **and visible.** You get ahead here by being visible. Those who wait for recognition will likely wait forever. It's important to be hard-working and competent, but it's at least as important to be politically attuned.

Be on the lookout for the various "items of faith" that operate in your organization. You may find them in the messages that float in the collective unconsciousness of the group, as well as in the jargon, employee handbooks, mission statements, and the like.

Be alert also for subtle dissonances between what the key people say and what they actually do.

The articles of faith in my organization:	The reality:

6.2   Is a secret, coded "quasi-language" used here?

Many of the most important communications within organizations may be carried by nuance and symbol. Some people learn to function within that coded language. Others remain oblivious that the coded language even exists.

"From the things he didn't say, we learned what he did in effect say, and from that what he really did want done."

Upper level government manager, speaking of a previous boss

Another government manager put it this way:

"You have to look at both what is stated and unstated. You need to be able to look through the surface appearances to find the real objectives and values of the organization and to be able to deliver on them.

"What makes it even more challenging is the reality that in a government or political organization these values may be in constant flux. That means you have to be sensitive to rapidly changing perceptions. If you're not able to pick up on these, then you're labeled unresponsive.

"When you get near the policy-making level, the key is how comfortable those above feel in dealing with you on these unspoken values. If you have to ask for clarification, something's wrong. You have to be able to sense the second meanings behind what's said."

Communications may be intentionally murky—sometimes for self-protection and "deniability" if things go sour. Or what is said or done is left deliberately ambiguous, perhaps to test your astuteness, savvy and ability to fit in with the governing elite.

The unspoken messages may come as what seem to be jokes. The jibes about your bright ties or cluttered desk may carry as a second message a warning that you're not fitting in, that your dress is inappropriate to your position, or that you're not projecting the desired image of unruffled competence.

Coincidence or code?

Some coded messages may appear to be mere coincidences, meaningful only to those who have learned the key:

"Looking back now, I can't believe how much time my old boss spent deciding who was going to have the offices closest to his own office. He was the partner-in-charge, and called all the shots. Those placed physically closest would be the people he liked the most, or who were the strongest politically. He would put them close to himself so he wouldn't have to walk far to chat with them.

"Naturally the other staff members learned to read the signals: The managers or partners placed on the other side of the building were out of favor with the partner-in-charge. That's how you learned where you stood: when you got the word to pack up and move your office.

"It was the same at parties. He always took a long time going over who he would have sitting together. The rest of us learned to read the political implications of who was placed where.

"He put fast-trackers and the most interesting people with the best partners. Those who were going to be promoted that year would be seated with the highest-ranking partners. People who were out of favor, or whose spouses didn't have political connections, or were boring, got stuck together at tables off in Siberia."

Former Special Assistant to Partner-in-Charge,
Washington office, major consulting firm

Look back over some recent events in your organization in which people have been subtly moved in or out of favor. What overt or subtle signals communicated this, before or at the time? Record your insights on the template below. Add other cues later as you spot them.

The change that occurred:	The cues or signals that passed the message:

The hidden costs of coded communications

Managers who communicate in code generally end up promoting paranoia at the cost of productivity.

Once that kind of atmosphere builds, office Kremlinologists waste a lot of productive hours trying to decode the meaning of signals and non-signals alike.

Bottom line: managing by winks and nudges and secret codes is neither a useful nor effective method of running an organization.

Summary

Question 6

Am I attuned to the "real rules" that operate here? Is "disinformation" part of the way of life?

6.1   What are the professed "articles of faith" here? Does the reality differ?

6.2   Is a secret, coded "quasi-language" used here?

Question 7

Am I focusing my time and efforts on the ends that matter most?

> *"No one here tells me what my job is about, what the important objectives are. They just keep giving me more and more things to do."*

> Production manager, small consulting firm

How could someone *not* know what their job is about?

It's easy. Sometimes new tasks get passed down the organization chart until they stick somewhere. (In many cases, if anyone were to take a really fresh look, they'd realize that maybe those tasks don't need to be done at all.)

Or someone takes over a position, and does exactly what the previous job-holder did, and *only* that—nothing more or less, nothing innovative, nothing to advance the organization.

Over the years, different people keep on doing the same job in the same way—without anyone ever asking why. Or even asking whether what's being done in that job really needs to be done, or done as a priority.

Or the job changes as needs change, but the person in the job fails to adapt and just keeps on doing the old job in the same old way.

Or a person is promoted to a new job, yet keeps on doing that same old job in the new office:

"We have a group of managers here with whom we're having a real problem. They're people who were very successful in field operations, and we rotated them here to corporate headquarters to give them a wider perspective.

"The trouble is, they just can't seem to adjust to working in the headquarters environment. They keep trying to do the old job in the new role, and it doesn't work. Unless they learn to adjust, they're at the end of the line with this company. We can't afford to carry them if they're not doing today's job."

Corporate Personnel Director

One organization discovered it was having a problem when its top aircraft mechanics were promoted to supervisory positions. Some of these new supervisors still saw the job as about crawling into the engine, getting grease on their hands and feeling they're "doing something worthwhile, not just pushing paper."

Understandable, sure. But it fails to grasp the implications of why they were promoted into a supervisory role: so they could spread their savvy and know-how to other, more junior people needing guidance and distilled experience.

Similarly, when a good sales person is promoted to a sales manager slot, often the hardest thing is to sit back and simply *observe* during a sales call. It's hard to resist taking over the call "to make sure we didn't let a sure sale slip away." But the manager's job is to develop and manage sales people, not to salvage calls.

Job descriptions may be "mis-descriptions"

A job is not like a room, boxing you in. Even in the most rigid bureaucracies, you can usually push those walls back to do what really needs to be done, or to do it better.

"Too many people feel constrained by their job descriptions. They make the assumption that the job description boxes them in, and draws a line beyond which they cannot venture.

"The really effective people make the opposite assumption, that they are free to do anything that's not specifically excluded. These are the innovators, the movers-and-shakers, the people who cause good things to happen for the organization and themselves. To a new person, I say, 'Don't limit yourself, because there are far fewer limitations than you think.'"

Corporate Vice-President

Checklist: why you can't trust your job description

- Written job descriptions are usually vague.

- Even clearly-defined jobs may mean different things to different people. One librarian, in a classic example, may see the job as mainly "about" providing services to users, while another may see it as about maintaining order and enforcing rules.

- *No one* may know what the job should be about—especially if the job is new, or has never been performed well.

- Almost always, there will be far more to do than time or resources allow, so defining the job becomes a matter of choosing what *not* to do.

- Jobs grow as more tasks are added. Jobs change as the organization's needs change. But no one may have updated the job description.

7.1 In assessing whether you are focusing your time and efforts on the ends that matter most, ask,

– What was this organization set up to achieve?

– Are my efforts in fact making a significant contribution to that?

"The important issue of any job is to find something useful and constructive to do. In other words, to find ways in which you can add true value. In order to find what is constructive, to find what needs to be done, keep asking questions like, 'What is this organization really about? How does my department contribute to that? How does my job contribute? What other things could I be doing that might help this department in doing its job for the organization?'"

Up-from-the ranks Corporate Vice President

As you do this assessment, mentally draw upward to look from the perspective of what the organization as a whole is trying to accomplish, and identify the ways in which you can contribute true value to that effort.

How can you tell if you are contributing "true value?" Consider true value as anything that adds to the value of the overall effort. If you work for a car company, designing a better door handle contributes true value; attaching that handle right the first time contributes true value; sending a blizzard of memos to get staff added to your private empire does not.

In a government agency, finding a way to make the delivery of services faster, friendlier, and more efficient does contribute value; fighting turf battles with other departments does not.

If you're in sales, pulling back now and then to assess which are the 20% of customers who tend to contribute 80% of profits does contribute value, while just working through the same old customer list, in the same old way, probably does not add much additional value.

> *"I was 23 when I first started working for the government as a GS-3 file clerk. In 14 years, I made it up to GS-15, at the age of 37. I did well, and I'm proud of what I did.*
>
> *"To those who find themselves feeling boxed in by the GS ranks along the way, I'd say this: Find a way to get the job done. Don't just say it can't be done. Come up with a positive way to get it done. Keep saying, Let's see how we can make it work.*
>
> *"I saw it as my job to navigate around the rocks, and accomplish what needed to be done, not stand on the shore and complain about what a nuisance the rocks were."*

Agency Executive Officer, Federal Department

7.2 Are there productive ways in which I can expand my contribution?

You can generally "get by" in most organizations by meeting the minimum expectations of those who are buying your services.

But there's a problem: That minimum is good enough only so long as the market remains in your favor.

Additional problem: In many markets, "New!" "Better!" "Improved!" are always happening. (Or at least being claimed.)

"Minimum expectations" means performing the expected job in the traditional way, keeping within the apparent boundaries, doing what your predecessor did, and adding none of your own initiative or creativity.

But this kind of passive approach carries long-term costs. To be *average* means being *stuck back in the pack*.

"I find that all too many people just fill a chair and wait for the job to come to them. Instead, from the start, I made a conscious effort to go out to the job, asking "What's in the best interests of my organization, and how can I help to facilitate this?" From that, everything else flowed."

Ambassador, U.S. State Department

"One needs to learn to push the boundaries of the job—at least the artificial boundaries. Push the artificial boundaries, but respect the real boundaries. Don't overstep the real boundaries.

"How do you distinguish a real boundary from an artificial boundary? To give an example, it would not be appropriate for me to undermine my counterpart in another division. In that respect, the division between his area of authority and mine is a real boundary, and it wouldn't be appropriate for me to push that.

"What I look for is a person who views the job description as the minimum, and so is always pushing outward, looking for additional ways he or she can help the organization achieve its mission.

"But there is a fine line that needs to be drawn. Do push the boundaries of the job, but at the same time don't let yourself get bogged down in trying to straighten out other agencies or other people. You can't be in charge of the whole world. Move as broadly as you can in what is basically your area, but don't get so involved in other responsibilities that you fail to take care of your own."

Senior Federal Manager

Checklist: expanding the job, pushing the boundaries

- What are the "traditional" or commonly-accepted boundaries of my job? (These may involve authority, responsibility, freedom to innovate, take action or make decisions, or perhaps to slightly bend the organization's rules and policies to keep customers or clients satisfied.)

- How flexible are these boundaries? Are the boundaries real, for sound reason? Or are they only the result of inertia, habit, unexamined assumptions, and the like?

- Are there ways in which I can expand my job and produce new value to the organization? Particularly, what could I do that needs to be done that no one has done . . . while still doing my "customary and expected" tasks as well as ever?

- What is the worst thing that could happen to me or the organization if I push through these assumed boundaries and take on some of the potential new areas? What is the best thing?

- Caution: think first about how you can improve _your_ area of responsibility before trying to mind your co-worker's business.

7.3 Given the real-world limits of time and resources that exist here, what should I _not_ be doing now . . . or at least not as priority?

You can't possibly do everything that you _could_ on the job, and you certainly can't do everything _perfectly_.

It's easy to get caught up in trying to get the usual stuff done and to keep the in-basket empty, only to find, at the end of the day or month, that the important stuff has been overlooked. It needs to be your choice, and not the running out of the clock, that determines what does and does not get done.

"Each day I have to make a judgment on what I'm going to neglect. You can't do everything. Sometimes you just have to toss things and hope to hell they don't come back and haunt you. To survive, you have to "prioritize your neglect.""

Senior scientist, Federal Agency

Time and energy are finite resources, so what you choose *to do* closes off the other possibilities of what else you *could do.*

In business-school jargon, that's termed "opportunity cost." Whatever you do takes time, energy, and resources . . . which you gain by not investing it in other opportunities.

What you *are* doing may be more important than what you *could* do, or vice versa. But that should be a decision you make in a conscious way, not just let happen by default.

Is keeping the in-basket cleared what really matters most? That feeling of being all caught up is satisfying, but the "opportunity cost" of keeping current with the incoming is that truly important things may be neglected. Is responding to the crisis of the moment causing you to neglect more important possibilities?

"You've got to be knowledgeable enough about your business so you can decide your own priorities, because you're going to be behind on something damned near all the time."

Research veterinarian

The career costs can be serious if you let yourself get trapped into doing the wrong things:

"When I started in the job, I realized it was important to keep close tabs on the financial operations. I didn't enjoy that aspect, and wasn't particularly good at it. But it seemed essential not to let the finances get out of hand. Looking back, I see now that I should have farmed that work out to someone skilled in the area, but it didn't occur to me to do that at the time.

74

"It began to get worse as the Center expanded. Then the financial work suddenly mushroomed and began taking more and more of my time. Unfortunately, I still wasn't smart enough to find someone to delegate it to. I just labored on, putting in more overtime trying to keep up with everything.

"Around that point, the Board decided to begin a new fund-raising drive. That was something I really wanted to be part of. But the Director brought in someone else to handle that, because by then it was apparent that all my time was taken up keeping track of the day-to-day financial aspects.

"Ironically, I had let myself get tied up in an area that I didn't like and wasn't very good at, only to find myself locked out from something I really would have preferred and been much more successful in.

"But there was another negative, as well. Because I was constantly involved in the financial details, the Director began to see me as just a detail person. Until then, he'd been helping me grow in the job, but from that point, his perception of me changed, and I found myself locked into one very limited role in his mind.

"Looking back, I see now how all of that could have been avoided simply by concentrating on what I was best at and delegating the other."

Administrative Manager, Washington think tank

7.4   Is what I am doing now (both at this particular moment and overall) genuinely constructive, or am I just keeping busy?

"It's been my observation that we rarely get the time to do really useful things because we spend so much our time doing

inane things . . . and we do the inane things simply because we never step back to ask 'Why?'"

Corporate Vice-president

"Overhead" activities tend to take on lives of their own.. Planning and preparation and gathering materials and information and keeping up with the professional literature are important. But sometimes "getting ready" to do work gets in the way of the real job getting done.

Example: Every month a 30-inch stack of professional magazines and newsletters arrives on Jack's desk, and every month he gets through every single one. If anything is happening in the industry, he wants to know about it. He carries some of them home at night, and others on business trips.

Bill, in an office down the hall, gets the same stack of readings. But he made the decision that his job was primarily about developing products, not wading through literature. He scans the magazines for fresh ideas when he has time. But if he doesn't get the time, he tosses them and moves on. He knows he misses some developments, but to him the important thing is that his work flows out . . . and the cash flows in.

Here's a tool for pulling together insights from items 7.1–7.4.

Things I do at work in a typical day or week:	Value 1-10:	Likely worst case if I don't do this, or don't do it thoroughly:	What other more productive uses I could make of this time and effort:	Value 1-10:

7.5 If I were doing this work as a self-employed entrepreneur, not an employee, what would I do differently?

Even if you find yourself behind a desk in the bowels of the world's most hide-bound bureaucracy, it's nonetheless a helpful exercise to consider what you would do differently if you were doing that job as a self-employed person.

Actually, taking a fresh look at your job as if you were an outside contractor is not so fanciful as it might seem, given the fact that more and more jobs are being outsourced to contractors and free-lancers.

What if you were working on a month-to-month contract, dependent on the value—and *perceived* value—that you contribute? In other words, imagine that your *job* were in fact your *business*, so you had the responsibility of keeping your client satisfied and willing to keep on paying for your services, and maybe even send along new customers.

- If that were the case, *what* would you do, and *how* would you do it?

- What would you *do differently*? The same?

- What would you *not do*?

- What would you *do instead*?

- What steps would you take to keep that client aware of the value you're contributing? That is, What "public relations" work would you do on your own behalf in order to make yourself more visible, and to showcase the value of your work? What networking?

- What, if any, "political stuff" like joining the group for lunches, coffee breaks, after-work socializing?

- Bottom line: What implications? What does this look at your job from the perspective of an entrepreneur tell you about what you can do differently and better?

Checklist: viewing the job from the viewpoint of an entrepreneur

- *Who is my key client?* (Your supervisor on the job may be your key client, but then again someone at another level may be the one you really need to satisfy. Or it could be someone *outside* the organization—possibly the organization's key client— who may be the ultimate judge of your effectiveness.

- *What is the most valuable thing I can do for this key client (or clients, plural)?* Your direct supervisor may want things done by the book. But maybe you can help the ultimate client—and hence help your employer—by finding a way to cut the red tape in a special case.

- *What can I do to make my work output unique and increasingly valuable?* "Product differentiation" is a buzz-word in marketing—offering unique value, quality or whatever to make one product stand out from the competition. How can you "differentiate" yourself on the job? (Hint: the best way is to add special value of some kind or another. We'll look at how to do that in the next question.)

- What can I add to the service or product I deliver to make that key client willing to pay more for it? That is, is there a way I *can add value to the results* of my efforts?

- *What special talent or creativity can I bring to my work in order to make my contribution unique in all the world?* (Maybe what's really distinctive about you is your not-so-glamorous talent for hard work and the ability to get things done. *That* is unique! Use it!)

- *Overall, how can I add greater value to what I do?* What perhaps small but useful services can I add? What creative, innovative ideas extras can I offer?

One caution: An early reader of this book told of an up-and-coming accountant in a big firm who always put the client first, sometimes not charging for small tasks, or not billing for phone advice. The clients were happy, and they kept asking him back for follow-on assignments. But the senior partners in the firm were not so happy, and the young guy was passed over when his time to make partner came. He moved on to another firm. Question: Were the partners short-sighted, or prudent?

Summary

Question 7

Am I focusing my time and efforts on the ends that matter most?

7.1   In assessing whether you are focusing your time and efforts on the ends that matter most, ask,

> – What was this organization set up to achieve?

> – Are my efforts in fact making a significant contribution to that?

7.2   Are there productive ways in which I can expand my contribution?

7.3   Given the real-world limits of time and resources that exist here, what should I *not* be doing now. . . or at least not as priority?

7.4   Is what I am doing now (both at this particular moment and overall) genuinely constructive, or am I just keeping busy?

7.5   If I were doing this work as a self-employed entrepreneur, not an employee, what would I do differently?

Question 8

Am I learning from the right role models?

"When I came here to the research center, I identified those who appeared to be the most successful. I made a point of meeting them and watching how they operated. I made a point, too, of going to them to get their advice and counsel—what to do, what not to do, and the way to go about it."

Senior Scientific Researcher

Consciously, or not, we've all developed a personal style or pattern for approaching life and work.

In part, that pattern flows from personality factors, in part from early life experience, in part also from the examples of family members, teachers, mentors, and other role models. (Or sometimes *anti-role* models which we have rebelled against, consciously or not.)

That "style" serves as a useful template for how we react and work, so we don't need to come up with a novel approach for each situation.

But it's not good if we become totally locked into one set of approaches, mind-sets, and expectations, unable or unwilling to change when circumstances suggest the old pattern isn't working any longer.

Old dogs can learn new tricks, and we can learn more than one way to "be" who we are. A new model may be necessary especially when you move into a new job, or new organization.

How to get fresh approach and perspective

Ideally, you'll find yourself a mentor, a savvy old hand.

But what if there you can find no appropriate mentor? Then develop "virtual mentors" by studying the people who seem to be outstandingly successful in your field or your organization, and modeling on the approaches that have made them outstanding.

- The effective people have typically gotten where they are partly by talent and hard work but also by their astuteness in recognizing and providing the skills, behaviors, work outputs, and even speaking style that are perceived as important in that company or line of work.

- Another advantage: people tend to hire and promote in their own image. Thus the present leaders are more likely to recognize excellence if it arrives resembling them in vocabulary, attitudes, approaches, and even dress. By modeling on the present and future leaders, you increase your chances of becoming visible to them in a positive way.

- That does not mean cloning yourself on them, or aping their every mannerism. You are who you are, but you can *expand* who you are by learning from them. It does mean making an effort to think in tune with them, and to project the kind of image and energy with which they are familiar.

- It also means making the effort to anticipate and ask the kinds of questions they would ask, to be attuned to the kinds of signals they send, and to approach projects with the kind of practical mind-set they likely demonstrate.

Reverse engineering

Maybe you don't like the idea of "role modeling" on mentors. Maybe it reminds you too much of little kids emulating action heroes or movie characters.

If so, then think of it as "reverse engineering." What's reverse engineering? When a break-through product comes out—maybe an exceptional new car model, or a computer, or some other gadget or high-tech tool—the competitors go out and buy a bunch of them, then turn their engineering teams loose to tear the product down to components and find precisely why it's good, and what the other company did to make it stand out.

If you don't want to role model on the stars in your organization or profession, then "reverse engineer" yourself, using them as your benchmark.

Whether you want to think of it as "role modeling," "reverse engineering," or "reconceptualizing" yourself, it's all comes down to the same thing: taking a fresh look at yourself and the way you've been handling things, then taking action based on what you learn from these models.

Use the questions and other tools that follow to help you gain perspective, and to put together a set of concrete strategies for implementing these ideas in your life.

8.1 Who are the people generally recognized as outstanding in my organization or profession? Why? What does that suggest?

Begin by listing the names of some of the people who are particularly effective and well-respected in your field.

At least some of these should be people with whom you work or can personally observe, so you see them in action, not just by reputation.

Checklist: Factors to consider in developing your list of role-model candidates

Some tips: As you look at your potential role-model candidates, look at their careers in a context broader than their present jobs:

- What did they do well before they stepped into this role?

- What helped them stand out early?

- Why were they promoted to this present job— what had they done successfully earlier to become visible?

- If they are self-employed, how do they catch the eye of potential clients? What do they do to instill confidence?

Other factors to consider in picking real or virtual role-model candidates:

- Typically, above-average abilities at the technical details of the job, but also other capabilities. (Maybe they are not only good technically, but also have unusually good interpersonal skills. Or the ability to communicate the techie stuff in a way that makes sense to others.)

- The ability to do well whatever job or task they undertake.

- Ability to spot the important things, and get them done.

- Ability to produce the kind of results that are valued by the organization or clients.

- Special ability to get things done, quickly, and without the need for continuing oversight.

- Ability to be good—perhaps even outstanding—at whatever job they have been given. That reflects, among other elements, flexibility and adaptability.

- Special creativity, directed in practical ways that advance the important needs of the organization.

- Flexibility: ability to adapt quickly to changing needs, and to the changing customs and "politics" of the organization.

- Political astuteness attuned to the realities of the organization as it is at the moment.

- Special "people skills."

- "Rainmaking" ability to attract new business or funding.

- The ability to project a sense of special competence, energy, enthusiasm, diligence, professionalism.

- Charisma.

The template below is a tool for developing and tapping the approaches of a "team" (real or virtual) of role models.

People who are especially respected, and/or have been especially well rewarded in that organization or profession:	Sum up, in a word or short phrase, the key skills that have enabled each to stand out. That might be technical, interpersonal, political, other . . . or a combination
1	
2	

8.2 Suppose these outstanding people now held my role or job: What would they do differently than I? The same? Why?

Visualize one of these outstanding people working at your present grade level in your present job.

(Alternately, develop a mental composite of these role models, and visualize them handling your job, working with the same kinds of constraints and pressures that you face, surrounded by the same cast of characters—same boss, same co-workers, same people you presently manage.)

Visualize that role model, or composite model, working through a typical day or week in your job. Look for answers to questions like the ones in this checklist that follows.

- What would they do differently than I am now doing? What would they do the same?

- Would they set and stick to different priorities than mine?

- Would they be less or more flexible? When? In what circumstances?

- Would they invest more time and effort than I do in areas not directly related to the tasks of the job, such as networking with others both inside and beyond this organization?

- Would they invest more effort than I do now in working the "political" areas for support and additional resources than I do? Would they spend time on "internal public relations" that I don't feel I have time or inclination for?

- How would they expand the job? That is, in what ways might they push the boundaries of the job? What new responsibilities might they take on?

- How would they go about broadening their skills?

- Would they exhibit different personality traits than I? Would they be more outgoing? Better listener? More focused? More poised? More of a "command presence?" Better eye-contact? Dress differently? Better posture?

- How would they publicize themselves and their achievements? (While it's not good to be too self-promoting, it's also a bad idea to let your accomplishments stay hidden.)

- How would they handle the time wasters that plague me, such as excessive meetings, or people who drain time and energy?

- Overall, from this exercise, what changes could I make to the job or how I do it?

- What does this comparison tell me about what I am already doing right?

8.3 What specific, practical action steps will I take in adopting these new methods into my own approach?

Here you take the next step, which is to develop a concrete action plan for translating these new insights into your daily habits.

In the left column of the template below, list the new techniques or approaches that you plan to focus on implementing in your behavior this week.

Then look ahead to the kind of typical situations you face where you will likely be able to exercise that skill or ability. Mentally rehearse in advance some typical ways in which you will employ it, so that you can be ready to put that into practice without fumbling.

Suppose you admire the role model's ability to mediate conflicts, perhaps in meetings. Thus, as an action step for yourself, note the

"Staff Meeting on Wednesday" in that second column, and jot precisely what, how and when you will intervene.

Role model's technique/particular strength	Specific ways I will demonstrate that in my actions this week:
Carol's ability to mediate conflicts.	At staff meeting on Wednesday, I will: --**Listen well**, taking active role in drawing out all parties. --**Rephrase** as appropriate to clarify differences. --**Lead each side** to give feedback on how they perceive the others' positions. --**Gain clear commitments** to narrow the field of differences.

Try it yourself, pulling together your insights from this and the other questions in this section.

Role model's technique/particular strength	Specific ways I will demonstrate that in my actions this week:

Summary

Question 8

Am I learning from the right role models?

8.1   Who are the people generally recognized as outstanding in my organization or profession? Why? What does that suggest?

8.2   Suppose these outstanding people now held my role or job: What would they do differently than I? The same? Why?

8.3   What specific, practical action steps will I take in adopting these new methods into my own approach?

Question 9

Am I engineering the conditions that lead to success? Or am I setting up for failure?

"Whether an individual has initiative or not usually depends on how many times in the past they have experienced success rather than failure."

Corporation Vice-president

One of my early projects was with an experimental federal program inside a state prison system.

The program director, Dr. John McKee, was a psychologist who had spent much of his career studying why some young offenders were able to turn their lives around, while others, with equal intelligence and abilities, became habitual "recidivists," going back to "the joint," time after time.

Dr. McKee's crucial insight was that the younger inmates (generally ages 18 to 23) *were in prison because they had failed at most everything they had ever attempted.* They had failed at school, at building friends and support systems. They had even failed at crime, as evidenced by the fact that they had been caught and incarcerated.

So, McKee asked, Was there a way they could learn to break out of that pattern of failure?

One of the keys, he found in the course of his research, was that those who succeed have clear goals realistically within their abilities, yet those are also goals that cause them to "stretch."

The result: succeeding at these stretched goals gives a sense of confidence that carries over to other aspects of life.

Success became infectious. These young inmates spring-boarded from small successes to larger ones, each time gaining more confidence that they *could* succeed, as well as insight into what kind of investment and focus success required.

Some had dropped out of school at the sixth-grade level, convinced that they were stupid. Failure had followed failure. Now, after time in McKee's program, they had suddenly discovered that they did have the ability to achieve the goals they set. That new confidence, along with some remedial skills in reading and basic math, enabled them to catch up on the education they missed, sometimes covering the equivalent of a grade year in a month, sometimes even less.

My point? You *can* engineer the conditions that set you up for success, or for failure. Here are some questions to consider.

9.1 Do I choose the right targets? Do I choose achievable goals?

"Roger" dropped out of a doctoral program in English literature, and found a job as a sales rep for a tech firm.

> *"I really enjoyed my first three or four months as a sales rep. Driving around the city making calls on people was a relief after all those years stuck in classrooms and libraries. I managed to write some orders in my first weeks, and I was hooked: selling seemed an easy way to make good money.*

> *"Then I went into a slump, and I got totally discouraged. Before long, I found myself knocking off after lunch in order to avoid more failure. I'd put in some time making calls in the morning, then go read in the park until it was time to check back in at the office.*

"But my manager, instead of firing me as he could have, did a fantastic thing. He forced me to `taste blood.' so to speak. He prodded me and controlled me more closely, and coached me step-by-step. Gradually I began to accumulate a series of healthy orders, and I began to realize that I really could sell.

"Once I had tasted blood—that is, made enough sales to know that I could be successful—I regained my confidence and motivation, and it's been upward ever since."

Some questions to consider:

- What targets have I set myself in the past year?

- Have I failed to achieve any of these? Why? Looking back, were they actually achievable, or were they unrealistic?

- Again, looking back, how could I have adjusted my objectives to make them more achievable? Set different goals? Broken them into sub-goals? Used a different approach?

9.2 Do I engineer the conditions around myself and my work in ways that increase the probability and frequency of my experiencing success?

How do you go about "engineering" your success?

First key: Focus on goals that are achievable.

There's no benefit in having great, out-of-reach goals that you know very well are just dreams. The point is to set goals that you can achieve, thereby setting up a pattern of experiencing success early and often.

What is *achievable*? That depends on you: focus on setting some objective in your life that stretches you enough so that you get a sense of satisfaction when you have attained it. It should also be something that you can have a reasonably good chance of accomplishing, within a reasonable time.

For example, if you've never done any carpentry, then the objective to "build a cabin on our land by this time next year," is probably not going to be achievable by you at this stage—it's just too big of a first step.

Second key: Set goals that, while achievable, force you to stretch a bit.

While building that cabin is likely too big for a beginner to achieve, setting out first to build a picnic table is achievable, yet enough of a stretch if you're not quite sure which end of the hammer to hold. In short, at the start, set out on a project that is achievable, yet challenging enough to give you satisfaction of going beyond past limitations.

Third key: Allow yourself to feel the satisfaction when you do accomplish something significant.

Don't be in too much of a rush to move on to something else. Take a moment to feel the joy.

Checklist: How to convert actual successes into self-perceived failures

Note that this is a different kind of checklist: this is a *reverse checklist*, a checklist of the *things NOT to do*. That is, when you are managing other people *and if you want to* **demoralize** *them, do the following!*

- *Fail to set clear goals at the start*. That means that no matter how much you do accomplish it will still seem that there was more you should have done.

- *Judge yourself (or your staff) unnecessarily strictly*. Ignore the big-picture view of what you did accomplish, and how well you did it. Instead, focus on minor errors or imperfections.

9.3 Do I recognize—and draw strength and confidence from—my successes?

"The most successful people have a basic healthy self-confidence. They're able to draw strength from the record of successes that they have built up in the past. They know that even if they make a mistake in the present situation, it won't ruin them for life. This confidence comes through to others, and it makes the other people equally confident in them.

"The unsuccessful people tend to lack this basic self-confidence. They may have just as impressive a string of successes, but for some reason they can't draw on these successes for support. They overlook their proven record of successes, and see only impending disaster, because their outlook and expectations are negative."

Senior manager, international high-tech firm

How do you get that string of successes going, so that you can use that success-record to build from? Here's a checklist on that topic.

Checklist: Engineering for success

Do I consistently,

- Set clear, achievable goals?

- Choose the right targets?

- Set goals in "manageable increments?"

So, then, what is a "manageable increment?" It's a goal (or part of a larger goal) that you can reasonably accomplish, within a reasonable time frame. "Build a million dollar fortune" may be a laudable goal, but it may also seem overwhelming. It's too big a goal to build from. If, however, you break that into manageable chunks, such as "Have $20,000 invested by the end of next year, then that becomes a goal that you can achieve within a reasonably short time-frame. Then you can use that success as a self-motivator as you work toward other manageable increments of the larger goal.

Also, each manageable increment should be one that you have a high likelihood of being able to accomplish, yet which also "stretches" you enough so that you get a sense of accomplishment when you reach it.

- Make sure the goal is *significant enough—to me—to* be worth the effort it will entail?

- If success depends on the cooperation of others, do I communicate so strongly the expectation that things will get done that others will do their part that they are energized to act . . . now?

- Do I seize the initiative, if necessary? Do I use my ingenuity in setting up the conditions under which the inertia will be overcome?

9.4   Have I developed the mind-set of converting problems into challenges?

"The best thing a fairy godmother can put in a baby's cradle is a batch of difficulties to overcome."

Alfred Adler

"My boss isn't much of a manager, and spends as little time around the office as she can get away with. That makes it very hard to get decisions made when we need them, because even though she can't be reached, she's politically astute, and wants to have an input on everything, even the e-mails I send

to the coordinators we're working with in other departments. That makes it look like I'm the person who's holding things up.

"I've finally figured out a way to work around that. I simply wait till she is out of the office on one of those extended disappearances, and then I send the e-mails or make the final decisions that need to be done.

"I copy her in to what I've done with a memo saying, 'Since I couldn't reach you on Tuesday, I went ahead and sent this memo.' That way I've got it on paper that she was unavailable when needed, and she can't very well come back and complain without admitting she was goofing off somewhere unreachable."

Federal employee in the technical area

"A project has been hanging around for months, and just doesn't get to it. Meanwhile, I'm hung up, because I'm dependent on the results. So when I get back from this workshop, I'm just going to go ahead and take over the project and do it for him. It's a little more work for me, but until the project is complete, I can't really move ahead, anyway."

Mid-level manager, Federal law-enforcement agency

Am I facing a "problem," or a "challenge"?

It's not just a matter of semantics—it's a difference of world-view . . . and hence of expectations.

"Problems" are burdens. Problems are energy-drains. Problems are depressing to face.

But change the term and you change the perspective: "Challenges" offer opportunities to extend yourself, to test your limits. Challenges offer the chance to gain the kind of real satisfaction that comes from accomplishment.

(Granted, changing the term "problems" to "challenges" is playing with words, but aren't the words we use — and the mindsets they generate — what it's all about?)

List any "problems" you face:	Rephrase each as a challenge"

9.5   Do I move rapidly through my setbacks—AND my lukewarm partial successes—in order to find my real successes? Do I recognize when to cut my losses and move on?

Also,

9.6   If I am not committed to this project, why don't I just cut my losses and get out now, freeing myself to find something to which I can give 100%?

Determination, that never-give-up quality, is essential to success. If you're not able to push on through obstacles and dry-spells then you'll likely never work through to real successes.

But there *is* such a thing as *too much* determination. There comes a point when a sensible person realizes that pounding on the same door in the same way is just not going to work.

Nobody likes to fail, but worse than failing is fighting lost causes and hence losing out on the opportunity to move beyond to the successes that could be.

Lukewarm successes versus lost opportunity cost

Sometimes it's best to accept the fact that we've tried our best, but it's still not working — and is not likely to get much better.

Sometimes, too, it's best to accept that even things that *seem* to be succeeding might not be successful enough in the longer term.

Sometimes, even worse than failing is getting bogged down in a lukewarm success, and hence losing out on an opportunity to achieve a larger success that might have been.

"Opportunity cost" is one of those buzzwords beloved by economists and MBAs. In plain English, the opportunity cost of undertaking Project A is sacrificing what else you could have done if you had instead invested that time and effort in Projects B, C, or D.

If you're out in the dating world and keep going out with Jack (or Jacquie) who's comfortable but not really right for you, then the opportunity cost is that you miss the chance to come upon somebody else who might be better.

It's the same in careers and business. Sometimes it's best to lose in order to win: to pull the plug on Project A and move your time and energy to the opportunity in Project B. If you push on and on to avoid failure in Project A, you won't have the time or resources to undertake Project B.

"Procrastanalysis"

There's a saying going around, "If you're going to fail, then fail fast." The point is, don't sit on your hands endlessly analyzing something. Don't get bogged down in that fuzzy world between analysis and procrastination. Instead, make a start, try something, get a sense of whether it will fly or not. If it does not, then—with the time you've saved from over "procrastanalysis"—try something new . . . or even try the same in a different way.

The company that is Facebook started not so very long ago, and has grown fast. Some of the ad hoc philosophies as posted on the walls at Facebook's headquarters (as reported in *Fortune*):

One is, "Done is better than perfect."

Another: "Move fast. Break things."

The point is not to be careless, rather to get things out into the world and see if they work. If yes, then you can come back and fine-tune and clean up the details at a later time.

Checklist: assessing the value of Opportunity Cost

If you're stuck in a project, problem situation, venture, invention or whatever that's just not coming together, ask,

- Suppose I were to walk away from this — what else could I be doing with that time, money, energy etc.?

- What if I shuck off this old semi-failure (or semi-success) — in what new directions would I want to (and be freed to) move? Would that be better in the longer term?

- Is this present minor, or mediocre—but comfortable—success worth the opportunity cost? Is staying within this comfort zone causing me to sacrifice the chance to invest myself in something more significant, or that I care more about?

- Is pounding away at the same door in hope of finally getting through really worth the opportunity cost of losing out on what else might be waiting just inside a different door?

Summary

<u>Question 9</u>

Am I engineering the conditions that lead to success? Or am I setting up for failure?

9.1   Do I choose the right targets? Do I choose achievable goals?

9.2   Do I engineer conditions around myself and my work in ways that increase the probability and frequency of my experiencing success?

9.3   Do I recognize—and draw strength and confidence from—my successes?

9.4   Have I developed the mind-set of converting problems into challenges?

9.5   Do I move rapidly through my setbacks—AND my lukewarm partial successes—in order to find my real successes? Do I recognize when to cut my losses and move on?

9.6   If I am not committed to this project, why don't I just cut my losses and get out now, freeing myself to find something to which I can give 100%?

Question 10

Am I willing to trade my comfortable set of self-fulfilling expectations of limited success for more productive expectations that push me to risk and grow?

"To exist is to change, to change is to mature, to mature is to go on creating oneself endlessly."

Henri Bergson

"A pessimist sees the difficulties in every opportunity; an optimist sees the opportunity in every difficulty."

Winston Churchill

"To improve is to change, so to be perfect is to have changed often."

Winston Churchill

"If you are working in a highly competitive environment, you have to realize that you can't hope to win every time. While you shouldn't operate with negative expectations, you should nonetheless realize that the risk of a loss is real.

"This is important so you are able to bounce back when one of those setback comes. Don't let yourself become bitter at how others 'did you in,' or failed to keep their word and stand behind you.

"Understand that if you strike out once in a while it doesn't mean that you've become a loser for the rest of your life. Learn from setbacks, bounce back, give your full support to the winning ideas, and move on."

Claude Lineberry

It's safe, it's *comfortable*, to carry on in that zone where we know we can handle things without risking mistakes or encountering the fear of the unknown.

But there are short-term costs and long-term consequences from staying too much in the comfort zone: For one, others (particularly the people who hand out promotions and raises) take you for granted.

Beyond that, sooner or later you'll look back and realize that if only you had pushed your capabilities a bit further, you could have done much more, and had much more satisfaction.

10.1 Do I dare to extend my limits, and take the risk of setbacks?

Am I willing to trade my set of self-fulfilling expectations of limited success for more productive expectations that force me to risk and grow?

Am I willing to push beyond my present comfort level and present level of expertise into new fields that force me to extend myself, to risk . . . and hence to grow?

"In my role as a personnel manager, I see two types of people. Some are risk-takers, others are not. You see the difference in matters like applying for promotions, or moving among jobs. Some people don't want to move on to a new job until they have absolutely mastered the present one. Even then, they'll hesitate because they don't like the uneasy feeling of that period in the new job when they're not yet an expert.

"Those who are open to risk have a quite different attitude. They try to do their present job well, but they don't get hung up on becoming overly expert in it before they're open to moving on. They learn what is to be learned from a job, then are ready to move on and broaden themselves.

"They look ahead five or ten years and see the skills they will need if they are to be ready for the job they want then. They don't hesitate to take a job now if it will give them those skills—even though it means they have to live for a while with the stress of not being totally on top of the new job.

"The non-risk takers, on the other hand, are not prepared to live with rejection or failure. They fear these things so much that they avoid any situation that could lead to failing or to being turned down. They just won't put themselves out on the limb by applying for jobs.

"Unless you're a superstar, you'll probably get ten rejections on job applications for every offer you do get. You just have to accept the inevitability of rejections sometimes. It's part of life if you're going to break out of the cocoon. Recognize that if it's a good job, everybody is going to want it, and you're going to face healthy competition. We grow by challenges, so you can learn and strengthen yourself by facing that competition. We have to learn to accept set-backs, and bounce back if you don't happen to win this time."

Federal personnel officer

"Give every decision your level best. Try hard to get your ideas accepted. But if the decision goes otherwise—as a lot of them inevitably will—don't waste time complaining. Get busy helping to implement that decision."

Federal manager

Can you think of at least three ways you could experiment in pushing beyond what you have assumed are your limits—perhaps trying a new role, new approach, or taking up learning something new?

10.2   Do I dare to take risks . . . but *expect* to succeed?

"If I get one-hundred percent of my recommendations accepted, it means only that I've psyched out ' likes and dislikes. But that doesn't do much for the organization. It doesn't bring in the ferment of creativity. It only perpetuates the status quo."

Federal Scientific Manager

"When I'm in a group, I want to be the team leader, and I push for the job. I'm aggressive in getting that job. I think it's a good thing to be aggressive in a situation like that. If you aren't willing to take the responsibility, then no one will have the chance to recognize just how competent you are.

"It's like a baseball game. It's the last of the ninth, and everything is riding on the next play. You can bet that some players will be praying that the ball is not hit their way, because they're scared of making an error. But there are others out there praying that the ball is hit to them so they can be the hero. Guess which are the ones with the million-dollar contracts.

"Ultimately, it comes down to self-confidence. If you're always afraid of making an error, that becomes a self-fulfilling prophecy, and you inevitably will make that error. It's an absolutely sure thing, because you have as much as intended that error. But if you develop the ability to project self-confidence, even when you're a bit shaky inside, then that becomes a self-fulfilling prophecy, too."

Government Executive

"If you have tried to do something and failed, you're vastly better off than if you had tried to do nothing . . . and succeeded at that."

Unknown

10.3 Do I put my energy into being productive, not just into avoiding failure?

"In the course of history, the successful commander has been the kind of man who deliberately burns his bridges behind him to prevent thought of anything but victory."

General Maxwell Taylor

"Success is never final, failure is never fatal."

Winston Churchill

Is there some area of your life or career—or in the immediate task at hand—in which you have been more focused on avoiding failure than on accomplishing some important end? If so, how to handle it next time?

10.4 Do I understand—deep down inside—that I'm not the only one here feeling a sense of insecurity? Do I push on, regardless?

"Dave is our specialist in working with the top-level managers from our major clients. If we're on the verge of a major order, we invite their head honchos, the top-level decision makers, here to corporate headquarters for a demonstration. We send one of the corporate jets for them, and when they get here give them the full Dog-and-Pony show.

"Dave makes the presentation, and coordinates all the negotiations. There's enormous pressure, because so much is resting on this meeting. Depending on how they react to Dave's presentation, we either get or lose an order for several hundred thousand dollars, or maybe a lot more—more—one in which we have months and months of preliminary work invested.

"Before the presentation, you can sense how nervous he is. He doesn't let it show, but if you know him as well as I do, you can see the symptoms. Down deep, he's quaking in his boots, as anyone would under that kind of pressure.

"But he doesn't let it stop him. He's nervous, and he's probably saying, "If I only get through this one time I'll never get in this spot again." But he carries through and gives a masterful presentation, and next time volunteers to do it again."

Manager, Headquarters Staff, Office Products Manufacturer

Summary

Question 10

Am I willing to trade my comfortable set of self-fulfilling expectations of limited success for more productive expectations that push me to risk and grow?

10.1   Do I dare to extend my limits, and take the risk of setbacks?

10.2   Do I dare to take risks . . . but *expect* to succeed?

10.3   Do I put my energy into being productive, not just into avoiding failure?

Is there some area of your life or career—or in the immediate task at hand—in which you have been more focused on avoiding failure than on accomplishing some important end? If so, how to handle it next time?

10.4   Do I understand—deep down inside—that I'm not the only one here feeling a sense of insecurity? Do I push on, regardless?

Part three:
WHAT'S MY BEST MOVE AT THIS POINT?

In Part one, the focus was on cutting to the core of what game (or games) were being played.

We determined that by looking at these questions in the first group, the questions that addressed the issue of What's this Game About? Who Are the Players?

Question 1 How do *we* "win"? That is, "Where" do we want or need to be afterward, and how will we recognize that we've arrived there?

Question 2 Who else is involved in this "game"? What is likely to be their idea of winning?

Question 3 What's really going on here? Is this a real issue, or a subtle test?

Question 4 What is this situation ultimately about? Where is the crunch?

In Part two, still operating with that sense of "game" in mind, we drew back to see how we're doing so far, and what we might change in order to do even better. Use the questions in this Part to help you develop an objective, systematic methodology for assessing how you're doing, day by day, game by game, year by year.

Question 5 Am I being given the recognition and compensation that I *honestly* deserve? If not, why not?

Question 6 Am I attuned to the "real rules" that operate here? Is "disinformation" part of the way of life?

Question 7 Am I focusing my time and efforts on the ends that matter most?

Question 8 Am I learning from the right role models?

Question 9 Am I engineering the conditions that lead to success? Or am I setting up for failure?

Question 10 Am I willing to trade my comfortable set of self-fulfilling expectations of limited success for more productive expectations that force me to risk and grow?

Now in Part three, again with that sense of "game" in mind, we focus on tactics and strategies for winning the games we encounter. *In other words, Given where you find yourself positioned now, what is your best move from this point?*

Question 11 Is a confrontation really necessary? If yes, is this the best time and place?

Question 12 Do I really need to be involved in this? Is this really *my* problem? If yes, is now the best time?

Question 13 What should I be considering *before* taking action? Am I thinking enough steps ahead?

Question 14 What should I be considering *afterward*? What lessons did I learn from this?

Question 15 What's the best choice under these circumstances? Is this a decision I can defend?

Question 16. When I look back on this, what will I likely wish that I had done, regret that I had done, regret that I failed to do?

Question 11

Is a confrontation really necessary? If yes, is this the best time and place?

"Are we trying to take the beach, or win the war? Sometimes the two are in conflict."

> Manager, new ventures group, major international bank

Most of the time, the ultimate objective will be to engineer overall solutions, rather than to try to "win" each little squabble along the way. Trouble is, if you're in an organization where conflict and confrontation are the norm, then it's hard to break out of the "We really, *really* gotta win this one!" mind-set.

You know the drill. Ann proposes Plan A, and Bob champions Plan B. In reality, there's really not a whole lot of difference between the two approaches, except that Plan A is Ann's idea, and Plan B is Bob's, so it becomes a slugfest in the meeting. That drags the issue out to a second meeting, and maybe more after that. Meanwhile, a lot of other important things are put on hold.

Why this pointless fight? Because in that organization, the "culture" says that you've got to fight for your ideas, and that if you lose on any issue, then you lose credibility, perhaps permanently.

But that may be just the *accepted* wisdom. Even when it seems that "fighters" get bonus points, the *truth* is that most others get fed up with the pettiness, and respect those who can move on and *get things done.*

True credibility comes from winning the *important* confrontations— the ones that matter, on issues that matter.

In determining whether this is a time to confront or to "chill," consider questions like these:

11.1 Is a conflict taking place, overtly or covertly? What is it really about?

The word "conflict" covers a lot of ground, from mild disagreements to competitions to quarrels and angry words and even shouting matches and tantrums.

Conflicts are not always overt; sometimes they take the form of subtle, quiet, covert clashes that take place out of sight.

Conflicts can be good. After all, if we all thought alike, there would be no innovation. Conflict spurs creativity and fresh thinking.

But that presumes a clear conflict, where all parties know what is really at issue . . . and where all the parties are direct and honest in their positions. (And, needless to say, where the subject of the conflict *matters*—that is, it's about significant things, not just personal egos, empire-building, and the like.)

An environment where conflicts and competitions simmer beneath the surface for long periods of time, with subtle battles being fought from time to time, is a breeding ground for counterproductive paranoia. (Of course *you* already know that, but some bosses just never learn!)

11.2 Will going into a conflict mode here and now really help me accomplish my ultimate objective?

This echoes Question 1 way back at the start of this book: *How do we win? How will we measure success?* That is, "Where" do we ultimately want to be when this is finished?

Sometimes your objective *will* be to establish that you're as tough as any of the other kids in the class. Remember how things went a lot better back in grade school once you stood up to a bully? It's much the same in some supposedly-adult organizations.

Sometimes you do need to make the trade-off: That is, to be prepared to "waste" time and energy on an otherwise pointless confrontation now in order to establish your toughness or credibility, and to clear up any doubts about how "strong" you are. "Credibility" translates into factors such as whether you're really listened to, and hence whether you get what you need.

> *"There is a secret that no one has told you: Real life is junior high. The world that you are about to enter is filled with junior high, adolescent pettiness; pubescent rivalries; the insecurities of 13-year olds; and the false bravado of 14-year olds."*
>
> Former NBC anchor Tom Brokaw. Commencement speech.
> Emory University, spring 2005

Sometimes it is necessary to be a squeaky wheel. Sometimes you do need to be pushy, maybe even flat-out confrontative. There are times when it is necessary to demonstrate toughness if you're to be listened to, to get what you need now, and to establish your credibility in the future.

11.3 Suppose I "win" this conflict—what do I gain? Suppose I "lose"—what likely consequences, both immediate and longer-term?

Sure, it's nice to come out on top, to gain the reputation of being "tough," "somebody not to be pushed around," "a winner every time."

Ah, but does winning *this* one really matter? What will you actually have gained—apart from the sense of victory? Will this be only a hollow victory that doesn't really change things?

Beyond that, what would be the *costs* of winning? Suppose you win here, who might you antagonize? What risks and obligations are you taking on? How would it impact your future relations with people around you?

Is that the reputation you really want among people with whom you will continue to be living and working? That you are "tough?" "Hard-nosed?" "Uncompromising?" Or, "Overly-aggressive?" "Combative?" "A trouble-maker?"

In some cases, "combative" or "tough and uncompromising" *may* be the reputation you want to develop. It depends on the organization, the "culture" within it, and the specific people with whom you will be working.

On the other hand, just suppose *what if* you do lose here? Or what if you simply concede this issue and let the other parties get their way? What have you really lost?

Maybe it would be only a symbolic loss.

Would fighting on really be worth the cost and effort? Would it be worth antagonizing others?

Regarding . . .	If I win, precisely what is it I win?	If I lose, what have I really lost?
My reputation?		
My relationships with others, including people, departments, etc.?		
Longer-term: such as additional work, risk, responsibilities?		
Gains: e.g. budget, staff. Maybe a promotion or better visibility?		

11.4   If the conflict is both real and significant, is now in fact the best time to deal with it?

Putting problems off till another day is *not always* a bad strategy; a lot of problems and conflicts do in fact resolve themselves . . . or at least become less pressing.

On the other hand, sometimes conflict situations fester and get worse if left unresolved. Sometimes the stresses of procrastinating— and worrying about what's likely to happen—outweigh those of just dealing with it and moving on.

"If you anticipate there's eventually going to be a problem situation or conflict, then, as a rule, the sooner you can cause it to come about the better. That way, you can deal with it earlier and get past it. You have more lead time. You're not so likely to be caught in a time crunch. Most important of all,

you get to choose the time and place, so you have home-field advantage."

New ventures manager, International bank

Checklist: When and when best to deal with a conflict

- Is there any good reason NOT to deal with this situation now and get past it?

Some situations do resolve themselves. People leave or wise up, or the pressure eases, or the dispute goes away.

But an unresolved situation may be an irritant, draining your energy just by being there. You may waste time rehearsing what you're going to do and say — energy and creativity that you could put into more productive uses if you just dealt with the situation ASAP and got past it.

- What is the best—and worst—thing likely to happen if I . . .

--confront now?

--*avoid a* confrontation at this time?

	Beneficial/positive effects?	Disadvantages/negative effects?
If I confront now?		
If I do not confront now?		

11.5 Is this a situation in which it's best to accept a strategic defeat—that is, to lose gracefully now, in order to be better positioned for the future?

"It's important to be willing to stand up for what you think is right, to be prepared to take people on when necessary. But you also need to know when you've lost the battle, so you don't waste your energy and credibility in fighting lost causes."

Senior manager, U.S. State Department

The key is learning to develop the ability to be a fully-committed advocate, but also retain the ability to detach yourself, mentally and emotionally, and move on if the decision goes another way.

"Give every decision your level best. Try hard to get your ideas accepted. But if the decision goes otherwise—as a lot of decisions will—don't waste time complaining. Get busy helping to implement it."

Federal manager

"We have endeavored to set up the decision-making process here so that everyone appropriate will be able to make their input, freely and openly.

"But once that decision has been made, we expect that they implement it. Without this sort of discipline and commitment, there would be anarchy within the organization. We can't go on discussing things forever. Once a thing has been decided, then that's it: we go do it."

President, Canadian subsidiary of international high-tech firm

But what if *you* are not the ultimate decision maker— that is, if you are not the person or team who actually makes the decision? Then your role is to make the best possible case in support of the position you recommend.

If you do that well, then you have done your job, regardless of whether the final decision goes the way you recommended. The fact that the decision happens to go against the position you advocated does not mean that you "lost," or that you or your advocacy has been rejected.

It's not personal; don't look on it as a rejection of yourself or your abilities. Management decision-making is mainly a matter of *balancing:* balancing the needs of one part of an organization against those of another, balancing the need for expansion against the realities of the budget available, balancing the need for fresh approaches and ideas against how much change and turmoil the people and organizational structure can take at one time.

You may have no idea what other concerns—or what "big-picture issues"—were in the decision maker's mind. Your presentation may have been impressive, and your argument compelling . . . except that there were more pressing needs that pushed the boss into making this choice. (Or maybe considerations of the politics within the organization had a key impact.)

> *"If you are working in a highly-competitive environment, you have to realize that you can't hope to win every time. While you shouldn't operate with negative expectations, you should realize that the risk of a loss is real. If you strike out once in a while, it doesn't mean that you've become a loser for the rest of your life. Learn from setbacks, bounce back, give your full support to the winning ideas, and move on."*

> Claude Lineberry, fellow consultant and old friend

> *"My boss is one of the most efficient human beings I've ever known. When you come to him and point out a mistake you think he's made, he's very quick to acknowledge it and move on other matters. If he thinks he's right, he'll counter and give you his reasoning.*

> *"But at whatever point he realizes that he's wrong, he immediately accepts what you're telling him, and doesn't*

waste any time arguing. He doesn't hold out for the sake of winning. He's interested in bigger things, not proving he's right on every issue."

Administrative manager, Washington research center

Tenacity is a virtue, but there's another side to that coin: We all have limited time, limited energy, limited resources — and limited time in a job before things happen and you either move up, or are pushed out.

Given these limitations, it's often best to cut losses early and not waste time and energy fighting lost causes. By cutting losses, we can move on and invest efforts in new areas, where the chances of success are higher. Maybe the question comes down to, How can I best invest my time and energy in pursuing success, instead of simply avoiding failure?

Checklist: Losing Strategically

- Keep your focus on the overall objective. What do you ultimately want to accomplish? Is winning this one here and now essential to accomplishing that objective?

- Support the winning idea and winning team, for the sake of the organization . . . as well as for your longer-term benefit.

- Don't sulk or quit. (Of course, *you* haven't sulked or taken your marbles and run home since age 10, have you?)

- Prepare to bounce back with new ideas and new energy, next time round.

- Move quickly past your setbacks in order to find your successes.

Summary

Question 11

Is a confrontation really necessary? If yes, is this the best time and place?

11.1   Is a conflict taking place, overtly or covertly? What is it really about?

11.2   Will going into a conflict mode here and now really help me accomplish my ultimate objective?

11.3   Suppose I "win" this conflict—what do I gain? Suppose I "lose"—what likely consequences, both immediate and longer-term?

11.4   If the conflict is both real and significant, is now in fact the best time to deal with it?

11.5   Is this a situation in which it's best to accept a strategic defeat—that is, to lose gracefully now, in order to be better positioned for the future?

Question 12

Do I really need to be involved in this? Is this really *my* problem? If yes, is now the best time?

Most people never need to go out looking for problems—there are usually more than enough already on hand. Problems are like germs, floating around in the air, looking for a warm body to land on.

Bottom line: Before adopting a problem, better invest the time to figure out whose problem it really is, and where it fits on the hierarchy of problems.

Types of problems to avoid

OPPs—Other People's Problems. *(Also known as BPs, Borrowed Problems)*

If it's not your problem, then why waste your time and energy in trying to solve it? Is taking on someone else's troubles really the best use of your time and energy?

UPs—Unsolvable Problems.

Not all problems can be solved. Some are just too big or too amorphous to be open to any kind of solution. Others are not yet "ripe" for solving.

Again, why spend your time and effort trying to solve the unsolvable? Better to invest that energy attacking problems where you can make a difference.

FP—Future Problems.

Sometimes it's a good idea to anticipate potential problems in order to avert them.

But not always. Sometimes problems resolve—or redefine—themselves. If you just steer clear, and exercise patience, they may go away. Or maybe what will work best is a little nudging, not a full press for the total solution, now.

It seems that some people don't have enough problems on their plates, so they reach ahead, borrowing from the future things that may never become real problems. Moral of the story: don't let *their* panic suck *you* in.

SSP—Self-Solving Problems.

Some problems are best left alone. Many will resolve themselves, one way or the other. Others will probably just fade away.

So before investing in trying to solve any, explore whether maybe it's best to just walk away and leave them, at least for now.

Types of problems that are worth addressing: When it is your problem, and when you can make a difference

The questions in this chapter serve as a checklist for making sure you're spending your resources on the problems that can make a difference.

12.1 Whose problem IS it? Am I necessarily involved?

Suppose (as happened to a friend) you're a teacher's aide, newly hired. It's your first day on the job, and the principal pulls you aside to "share some concerns." He informs you that the teacher with whom you'll be working can be "difficult," and that "you need to be ready to calm the classroom if she loses her cool."

You nod. "I'll do what I can."

Guess what? You've just adopted—or been delegated— somebody else's problem.

If that teacher is incompetent or unfit, then it's the duty of the *principal* to handle the issue.

The principal, after all, is part of management, and paid accordingly. But now that principal has abdicated that duty—by passing it on to you, along with the risks. If you handle it well, the principal can take the credit. But if an issue develops, who do you think will get the blame?

However, in other cases, it may not be your *own* problem, but may belong to someone so close to you that you are *necessarily* involved—maybe your child, or your employee.

Keep perspective: the problem belongs to them, not to you.

That in turn means that you can at best advise them, helping them to clarify the issue, and to generate some alternative solutions. (Of course, if you DO decide for them, or do take on some of the costs, then the reality is that you have just adopted the problem as your very own.)

Or suppose one of your peers at the job comes to you with a "situation" she says she doesn't know how to handle.

If you just give advice: then it remains an OPP—Other Person's Problem You give your input, and are free to carry on with your own job. If she still needs help, you're there to give further advice, if she asks.

But what if you say, "No problem, I'll handle it for you"? Then that OPP has become a YP—Your Problem—and it's likely to be the first of many that you inherit.

12.2 Is this really a problem that I (or we) should be investing time and effort in solving? If yes, is now the right time?

You can't solve every problem first—nor does it make sense to try, as the time and effort you invest in trying to solve something from the potential future will be taken from what is important to address now.

So what IS important to address now? It's helpful to ask these two questions:

First: Is this something that we have a reasonable chance of impacting now? Or is it a UP—Unsolvable Problem?

Not every problem *can* be solved, at least not to the satisfaction of all parties. Sometimes it's better to live with some situations and invest the energy in other ways.

Nor is every solvable problem "ripe" to be addressed now: Sometimes things really do need to get worse before the people involved get motivated enough to work together to solve it. Or for all the facts and implications to become clear.

If there's no reasonable chance of impacting (that is, solving or at least alleviating the problem now), then it is probably not worth the investment of your time and energy—certainly not at the cost of being drawn away from more significant issues that *can* be solved.

Second: What if we just leave it alone . . . at least for now?

> *"Nothing is sometimes a good thing to do, and often a good thing to say."*
>
> Will Durant, philosopher

When Garfield the cat sees a plate of lasagna, he just can't resist getting his teeth into it. A lot of 2-legged folks are like that, not necessarily with lasagna, but rather with problems.

That's a good trait, *sometimes*. Sometimes it's good to have the reputation of being an aggressive problem solver . . . someone who (in the jargon) "leans forward".

But not always. Some problems are like vintage wines whose time has not come. They need time to ripen so we can spot the real core of the issue.

Other problems—maybe even *most* problems—will tend to take care of themselves if left alone. They may simply dissolve, or they may change shape or urgency.

However, some problems can't be ignored, even though they are (a) not our problems, (b) are not particularly important, and (c) can't be resolved right now.

Those are like a leak in a boat that you've rented from somebody else—it's not your boat, it's just a tiny leak, you don't really have the tools to permanently fix the leak. But if you just let things go, you're going to be in deep trouble.

There's an important difference between procrastination (usually not a good thing), and "prudent inaction" (which can be very wise, at times). The template here helps you sort it out.

Reasons IN FAVOR of acting now:	Reasons AGAINST acting now:	WORST thing likely if I do nothing now:	BEST thing likely if I do nothing now:
1			
2			

12.3 Check: Is what I am proposing to do (or say) likely to help resolve (rather than complicate) the issue?

It's the weekly meeting in a regional branch office of a federal agency. Today's meeting focuses on progress in working with a private developer to put together a package for rehabilitating a block of low-income housing. Things have been stalemated for three months. The previous developer defaulted, leaving the government to carry the costs. Meanwhile the buildings sit idle, while the tenants wait for a place to live.

The Regional Director announces a new plan he has just put together to get the project moving again. Before he has finished, Richard cuts in: "It won't work, and I'll give you four big reasons why not. First . . ."

It turns out that Richard's "big reasons" are actually minor issues that he has blown out of proportion.

After the meeting, the Housing Director takes me aside and says, "Unfortunately, today's performance was typical Richard. He's a very bright guy, very capable in some ways. But he puts his energy into coming up with reasons why something can't work, instead of finding ways of making it work. Our job is to get housing built. That's what we're here for. Richard just doesn't grasp that. He looks on this job as an intellectual exercise, as if he were back in college debating philosophy."

To paraphrase that Will Durant quote above, *Sometimes nothing really is the best thing to say in meetings.*

12.4 Is there a practical, realistic way that I can—right now—cut through to bring the issue to some kind of closure?

It's *usually* a good idea to take the time to dissect a situation in order to overcome the Ready! Fire! Aim! syndrome.

But not always. *Sometimes* it is best to do *something*, even if that something is nothing more than make a start, even if it's not a perfect solution, or not perfectly thought through.

Sometimes just getting started helps clarify the issues, and clarify what realistic options are available.

Often, some practical closure—*now*—even if not perfect, is better than leaving things hanging waiting for the perfect, probably unattainable, solution.

Summary

Question 12

Do I really need to be involved in this? Is this really *my* problem? If yes, is now the best time?

12.1   Whose problem IS it? Am I necessarily involved?

12.2   Is this really a problem that I (or we) should be investing time and effort in solving? If yes, is now the right time?

12.3   Check: Is what I am proposing to do (or say) likely to help resolve (rather than complicate) the issue?

12.4   Is there a practical, realistic way that I can—right now—cut through to bring the issue to some kind of closure?

Question 13

What should I consider before taking action? Am I thinking enough steps ahead?

"Being a manager at the senior level is like playing a game of three-dimensional chess. You need to think about your present move, but also need to look ahead to see how that will leave you positioned for later moves.

"You also need to figure how your opponent—perhaps someone at another level in your agency, or someone in another agency, or someone in the media looking for a story—will likely to react this move.

"Meanwhile, you also need to be alert for tricks and traps the other players may be setting for you."

---Insight from a top administrator of a federal agency whom I interviewed in the course of conducting a management survey.

Here's another slant on the same theme, this from Walter Shapiro a few years ago when he was a columnist for *USA Today*:

"A true test of a . . . president is his ability to stay three or four moves ahead of the opposition. A president has to constantly calculate, 'If I do A, then Saddam Hussein will have to do B. Then I surprise him with C, and he's forced to capitulate with D.'"

Change the names, change the job titles, but it reinforces the point made earlier: That by drawing up to an above-the-board perspective, you'll find that the games — of politics, work and life —

make much more sense. From up-there, you may see that not only the *rules* of the game, but even the *real players*, may be different from what you're led to believe.

13.1 In this situation, what moves might I make? How would each of these potential moves likely play out down the line?

If Action A brings Desired Result B, that's good. Assuming, of course, that Result B is in fact appropriate here.

But before taking Action A, it's wise to think what other results might also flow from your action. What if it also brings Undesired Results X, Y, and Z, along with Totally Unexpected Results L, M, and O-No!

> *"You need to be able to develop a comprehensive picture of the overall needs of the department today, but you also need to be able to look down the road and think how the decisions you make today are going to affect your flexibility in the future.*
>
> *"For example, right now I need to hire some people. This particular job will change as we develop new computer capacity, and then we will need more professional-types who have more complete analytical skills. What I'm saying is that have to be thinking of the future mix of the people three to five years ahead as I make the hiring decisions for this year's jobs"*

Government executive

In looking ahead, consider questions like these:

- If I make the move that I am considering, what effects will likely result, both directly and indirectly?

- Am I looking enough steps ahead? Is someone else likely to be looking even more steps ahead than I am?

- What options will have opened up? What options will now be closed off?

- What am I opening myself up to by saying or doing this?

- How will this move be viewed by the others? How will they react or respond?

- How will they likely react? Try to help me? Block me? Stay clear of it?

- Is there any way I can make them more receptive in advance?

- If this is ever challenged, how will I explain or justify the action I am now taking?

- Double-check: If I take this course of action, will I be comfortable if my boss / my best friend / the media / my mom learn what I have done?

- What is presently unknown here, and what effects might result?

13.2 What unknowns and vulnerabilities lurk here? How can I prepare for and correct for them now?

As former Secretary of Defense Donald Rumsfeld famously put it,

"There are known knowns. These are things we know that we know. There are known unknowns. That is to say, there are things that we know we don't know. But there are also unknown unknowns. There are things we don't know we don't know."

Whether or not you're a Rummy fan, the point is well-taken. If you know the risks ahead, you're in good shape to proceed. But if you don't know what those risks might be, then pause to consider.

I'm by no means suggesting that you *expect* things to go wrong—because things tend to happen the way we expect.

Nonetheless, it's smart to look ahead, not to *expect* but rather to *recognize* what might happen, and hence to be pro-active in dealing with any key areas where we may be vulnerable.

- What are those areas? It all depends, of course, but here's a starter list, which you can add to from your situation and experience.

- What presently unknown (or unknowable) factors are lurking, regarding both things and people?

- What other "players" are involved in this? Do they succeed if we succeed? Or do they benefit (i.e. "win") if we fail?

- What might go wrong, cost more, take longer, break, get lost? With how serious an effect?

- What other outside contingencies may have an effect? (Think of factors such as delays in delivery of materials, delayed budget approvals, half-hearted cooperation by key players, etc.)

Then what? Then use the template below: First, list each unknown or each potential vulnerability. Then think through the possible consequences of each.

If the consequences seem significant, use the third column to begin an action plan for dealing with those risks.

Areas of vulnerability	What if this does not work out as hoped? Risks? Costs? Other?	Action steps I can take now to reduce the effect?

13.3   What mistakes am I at risk of making?

You might say, "If I'd *known* it was a mistake at the time, then, doggone it, *of course* I'd have done it differently!"

Sure. No doubt about it. We don't *choose* to make mistakes.

But a lot of mistakes come about simply because we don't start out looking far enough ahead. Here's a checklist to get you started.

What might I later wish that I had . . .

- Done differently?

- Thought through better?

- Done while I had the chance

- Done sooner?

- Not done?

13.4   What other games may be in play here?

Suppose you're trying to get your service business going—maybe as a consultant, interior designer, or website creator.

A call comes out of the blue from a stranger who says he's heard good things about you and your work, and wants to talk about your availability. "Can you come by for a few hours this week for a get-acquainted session? I'd like to draw on your expertise, see how we might work together."

That sounds reasonable enough. But if you're in a service business, then the reality is that all you have to sell is your time and expertise.

True, marketing is essential, but it's important to keep in mind that this caller may be playing a game, calling to tap the brain of an expert, though with no intention of actually *paying* for that expert's services. (And you may be only one of several experts he's playing that way.)

That's just one of several possibilities to be alert for before giving away too much of your time and expertise. Here are some others that could arise. (The point here is not to make you into a consultant, rather to get you thinking in this mode.)

- *Maybe this potential client doesn't know what he really wants. Or needs.* Which means you could end up spending a lot of uncompensated time cutting to the real issue, only to find that the issue may be something beyond the realm of what you can or want to handle.

- Or maybe the potential client does know what she wants, but *is missing the real issue*. If you proceed, and do it her way, there's a risk that the project may bomb, and at least some of the blame may attach to you, and cost you a chunk of your reputation. Beyond that, you might not get paid.

- Or perhaps the client has already wasted so much time and money on the project that it *cannot be done successfully within the remaining budget and time constraints*. She may have recognized this, and hired you with the thought that maybe you can work miracles. Or, if you aren't a miracle worker, then you'll serve as a scapegoat to take the blame.

- Maybe this would-be client is using the cover of the proposed *project as a cover for accomplishing something quite different than the stated purpose.* Maybe his underlying objective is to have you around to blame as the bad-guy in recommending some unpleasant or politically risky tasks that he doesn't want to be associated with. Or maybe he's hoping that he can engineer things so your recommendations undercut one of his rivals within the organization.

- Or maybe he does want to retain your services, but *the real reason is to use you as the villain.* Maybe he'll be asking for your input on what jobs should be eliminated. Then he can say, "Gosh, folks, this hurts me to have to fire you, but the consultant made me do it."

Granted, these are only possibilities—potential scenarios—but they are typical of the kinds of concerns to which it pays to be attuned— whether you're a consultant coming in from the outside, or a full-timer with perhaps even more to lose.

13.5 Whose input/advice/"buy-in" might I later wish I had gotten?

Suppose you're a junior manager, about to propose a change in approach for the organization. You give your presentation, feeling totally prepared — confident that you're going to shine, knowing you're about to step through the doorway of opportunity.

It comes off perfectly.

Except . . . except you don't get the support or enthusiasm that you'd hoped for.

Later, when you try to figure out why the support wasn't there, you realize that while the attendees mostly agreed with your proposal, they also may have been concerned because they were not sure of the implications for themselves and their roles.

Or they nitpicked to cover the fact that they had been caught unprepared for what you were proposing.

Or they held back until they could assess which ways the winds would blow.

Suppose, what if?

Things might have turned out better for you if you had invested some time earlier contacting key people, not so much to overtly pre-sell them as to ask their advice, with questions like,

- Any changes or refinements they would suggest?

- What would they change in your approach or the way you present it?

- Does it seem feasible? If not, why not?

- Are there any overlooked issues?

- Any "political" or "turf" concerns?

Not only would their answers have helped, and given you a chance for a pre-rehearsal, but they would have had time to think it through before the meeting. They might have made comments or asked questions to help you sharpen your responses, or anticipate any objections

First, you'll likely get some very good ideas from savvy people.

Second, (perhaps deviously), you may find that they become supporters because of the sense of "joint ownership" you've engendered by asking for their input.

What do I want to accomplish here? What problems am I trying to solve? That is, how do I "win", and how do I measure what winning means here?	
Who has experience or authority I could tap?	How will I approach and enlist their help or advice? Why is it to their advantage to do so?
Who might be threatened by what I propose?	Their likely concerns and how can I alleviate or defuse them?

13.6 Are any broader opportunities hidden within this situation?

In the mid-1950's, a family in California set up a successful hamburger stand marked by golden arches forming the M of their name, McDonald's.

Then a man named Ray Kroc drove by the place one day, and saw broader opportunities in what was already successful. He bought out the McDonald brothers, including the idea for those Golden M arches . . . and the rest is a case study in the archive of how one person can see opportunities that others don't.

- What am I taking for granted? If this is successful, what broader opportunities does that suggest?

- How can I capitalize on those possibilities? Can I do it alone? If not, who or what kind of help do I need?

- Is there an analogous situation with similar opportunities? What can I learn from it? What mistakes should I avoid here?

- Can I springboard from this idea or opportunity, and build on it, jump ahead, or whatever, to make it better?

13.7 If it's such good idea, why hasn't somebody already done it . . . and gotten rich?

A fabulous idea pops into your head, and you're eager to run with it. Before you run far, though, better ponder this question: If it is indeed such a fabulous idea, why hasn't somebody already run with it, and gotten rich? Or famous? Or whatever?

It may be that your idea is so original that never before has it occurred to anyone. If so, keep on running with it.

But then again, if you search around a bit, you may find that there really is something like it already out there.

That *may* be bad news—that there is existing competition.

On the other hand, contrary to what you might be thinking, it may actually be *good* news to find there already is competition. Why? Because that tends to indicate there really *is* a market for what you propose.

Beyond that, the competitors may already have done the heavy lifting of creating the awareness of a need for something like this.

Checklist: Has this already been tried? With what results?

- If so, has it made those other people rich (that is, successful using whatever measure matters here)?

- If not, why not? What can I learn from their failures?

- If it has made them successful, is there still room for me in this marketplace?

13.8 How can I make it "bulletproof?"

It's one thing to perfect and polish an idea, an invention, or a presentation.

- Making it "bulletproof" means going beyond just making it good. Making it bulletproof means investing effort in trying to anticipate all of the ways in which it could be attacked by competitors (or in-house nitpickers), then fixing those vulnerabilities.

- Suppose you have invented a new product or service. What additional aspects to that product or service can you add to make it less likely a competitor will come in and try to grab your business?

Suppose you need to make a presentation to senior management. What questions/concerns should you be ready for? From what agendas will others at the meeting be operating from/coming from? How will you prepare for those comments?

On the same theme, this from the CEO of Panera, in *Fortune*:

> *"These days I spend a lot of time thinking about how I'd compete with Panera if I weren't Panera."*

Do you spend enough time and energy thinking about how someone else might do your job better than you? Doing more of that might be a good investment of effort.

13.9 Can I "monetize" it?

"Monetizing" is MBA-speak. It translates as, "Sounds like a good idea, but can we actually make some bucks with it?"

Maybe there is hidden potential. Maybe with a few tweaks the basic idea can leapfrog to greater value, whether monetary or other.

Here's a mini-checklist of "monetizing" concerns to get you started:

- Is there a market for this? Do enough people have a need for this? Is that need strong enough for them to actually part with cash?

- Can we reach those potential users in a cost-effective way? No matter how many potential buyers there are, if those users are scattered then there may not be a cost-effective way of getting your advertising, word-of-mouth etc. to them.

- Can we make a profit?

- Overall, is it likely to be worth our time and effort? Is it a cost-effective use of our time and resources?

- Even if you're not doing it for a profit motive (perhaps it's a charitable activity), it's still wise to ask a form of the profit question—is the payoff worth the investment of time or energy, or is there something else that would be of greater help?

Summary

Question 13

What should I consider before taking action? Am I thinking enough steps ahead?

13.1 In this situation, what moves might I make? How would each of these potential moves likely play out down the line?

13.2   What unknowns and vulnerabilities lurk here? How can I prepare for and correct for them now?

13.3   What mistakes am I at risk of making?

13.4   What other games may be in play here?

13.5   Whose input/advice/"buy-in" might I later wish I had gotten?

13.6   Are any broader opportunities hidden within this situation?

13.7   If it's such good idea, why hasn't somebody already done it . and gotten rich?

13.8   How can I make it "bulletproof?"

13.9   Can I "monetize" it?

Question 14

What should I be considering afterward? What lessons did I learn from this?

"Failure is success . . . if we learn from it."

Malcolm Forbes

Once something is over and done, the inclination is to move on to the next item waiting on the agenda. It seems a waste of time and energy to go back over what can't be changed. Or it may be painful to dwell on something that didn't go well. But, as the saying goes. . .

"Hindsight gives 20-20 vision."

That's *usually* taken to mean that we can see clearly now what we *should* have seen earlier. But it also makes the point that looking back at what happened this time can give better *foresight* — that is, 20-20 vision when looking ahead to spot opportunities and pitfalls next time.

On the pages following are some questions for turning hindsight into futuresight.

14.1   What was I trying to accomplish here? Looking back, Was that the correct objective? To what extent did I succeed? To what extent did I fail?

Among the issues to consider here are these:

- Did I have a clear objective? Did I keep it clearly in mind?

- Did I take the time to think through all of the alternatives that were available then? (Or did I just go with the first idea that came to mind?)

- Did I invest enough time and thought back then in exploring or generating additional options?

- Was I at least partially successful? Did I succeed in achieving the most important part of the objective?

- Did I give enough thought up-front to things like how other people might react, or how going after this objective "cost" the chance to do other things? (On this, see Question 12, above.)

14.2 Did I get value from this? Did I *give* real value?

At the end of a project, or even at the end of a special day, I pause long enough to ask myself a pair of linked questions:

- Have I *gotten value* from this day (or this project)?

- But also, have I *given value* for this day wore this project?

The practice started at the end of one summer Saturday when I realized that I had mostly moped around the entire day. I had not done the weekend tasks that I had planned. I had not made the phone calls. I'd not gone for a bike ride or a swim. I had not read anything interesting.

In short, I realized that I had spent the day without getting value from it.

But, conversely, I also realized that I had not given value to that day. I had not been focused. I have not disciplined myself to focus on a project and bring it to completion. I had not even done any of the enjoyable things, like walking, biking swimming or reading because I failed to make the effort into focus.

Now I ask these questions which go together not only at the end of most days or weeks, but also at the end of projects.

14.3 What should I do differently—or the same—if I encounter this kind of situation again?

Sometimes things turn out badly, not because we made a mistake, but rather because of circumstances that existed at the time. Mortgaging the house to buy into the great tech surge was probably a good move in 1998, but not a couple of years later. Or buying a bunch of houses to "flip" might have been a good move in 2006, but again a disaster a couple of years later.

Tough if you lost money on the first, really tough if you got hit by both. But there was a lesson brewing the first time 'round: The warning pattern of Boom, Bubble and (beware of) Bust.

All of which suggests a couple of questions to consider.

First: *What other forms* might this same type of situation take? How will I recognize it if it recurs?

Patterns repeat, but often in not quite the same way. So, in analyzing what you did well or poorly in the previous case, give thought to what variations might arise. By spotting a similar pattern or variation early, you may be able to head off a problem, or recognize an opportunity.

Some typical patterns to avoid:

- Failing to ask the right questions, soon enough.

- Failing to push for solid, understandable answers—that is, answers that really make sense.

- Becoming mired in details and losing sight of the overall objective—or slipping off schedule or beyond budget in attending too much to relatively insignificant details.

- Trusting without verifying.

- Failing to react early enough when you sense that things are going sour, slipping behind schedule, or that the commitment of other necessary players is fading.

Second: If I see this pattern developing again, how should I move to keep this kind of difficulty from repeating? How should I move to seize an opportunity?

It's not enough just to recognize the pattern that has led to trouble in the past; equally important is to have a plan of action in mind so we can intervene early enough in order to cut off troubles before they develop.

Thinking through potential trouble scenarios provides a useful "mental rehearsal" so we can move quickly and confidently in adapting to what actually materializes.

Typical problem or opportunity within this pattern?	Did I handle it well? Mishandle it? How? Why?	How will I act if this, or something like it, comes again?

14.4 Suppose I had the chance to hit a go-back button and do this all over again . . .

- **What should I do the same?**

- **What should I do differently?**

- **What lessons flow from my answers?**

From the 1940's until he died at close to age 100, management guru Peter Drucker trained business strategists to focus on this question: "If we were not already invested in this business or this industry, would we move into it now?"

If the answer is No, then the smart move is usually to cut losses and get out now. If you wouldn't put *new* money in now, then why keep *old* money in? Money, after all, has the same value whether old or new.

Drucker's Question is by no means useful only in investment situations. Among the other ways you can use it:

Career path

If you had it to do over again, would you go to work in this field, or this job? If yes, fine. If no, then why put any more time in it now? Maybe you'll have to take a big pay cut if you switch, but, long term, how does that balance against being locked into the wrong path?

Self-employment

If you hadn't already quit that steady job and set up your own business, would you do it again, knowing what you know now? If not, then maybe you are postponing the inevitability of going back to a conventional job. Granted, you have now invested time, money, and maybe self-image in this venture, and it hurts to "waste" that. But if you wouldn't do it again, then why put more time in on top of what's already gone?

Hiring and firing

Think of an employee who you feel is presently underperforming, then ask, "If that person were now applying for the job, would I hire them?" If your answer is no, then is there any good reason not to let them go now, and find someone who is right for that job?

Granted, you may "feel sorry for them," or may "feel obligated." But maybe the best favor you can do is to set them free so they can move on and find the job for which they are a good match.

For that matter, maybe if they had it to do over maybe they would never have taken the job to which they now feel locked in. Maybe they'd fare best if you give them that nudge to attune to Drucker's Question.

14.5 IS there a way I can go back and remake that decision? BUT, would that be worth the costs? AND what other new opportunities would I be sacrificing?

Computers have a go-back button that lets us undo mistakes we make. What if there were go-back buttons for life-decisions?

Go-back and try again makes sense in *some* cases, but not in all. Living with the consequences of a bad choice—or just accepting it and moving on—might be better than the costs of undoing it.

First consideration: Time has passed since that decision, so we're not standing in exactly the same spot: Circumstances and needs may have changed.

Second: Every choice we make involves an opportunity cost. That opportunity cost includes the time and energy that we would put redoing the old project might well be better spent on a fresh new project. *Maybe* it is worth undoing this and doing it right next time round. On the other hand, maybe it's best just to live with it, move on, and invest that time and psychic energy in something new.

Third: There's no point in trying to erase handwriting that's already on the wall.

Finally: Persistence pays off . . . *most* of the time, but *not always*. Sometimes it's best to quit early and take your losses so you can reinvest your efforts in more productive ways.

Checklist: Looking back

- Is going back and trying to remake something from the past likely to be worth the trouble and expense?

- If I do go back and try to remake this past choice, what will be the likely effects on others? Will that frustrate them? Antagonize them?

- What have I actually *lost* by this past decision? Can it be regained?

- Have I, in some ways, actually *gained* from this loss or error? (For example, experience, wisdom, knowledge of what not to do?)

- Is going back really likely to be worth the opportunity cost? Or would it make more sense to put that time and energy into something new?

14.6 If I hear (or anticipate) criticism on this, what is likely to be the best response in this situation?

When things go wrong, some people will just want to vent. Others will claim that, if only *they* had been in charge this would never have happened. Still others will try dump the bad stuff on a scapegoat.

Yet, despite negativity and jostling for position, there may nonetheless be some valid ideas worth hearing and learning from. Even criticisms that are not well-intentioned may carry some productive advice.

Bottom line, a flexible approach is key when criticism comes. Choose your reaction (or mix-and-match) from these basic strategies:

Accept the criticism, and (maybe) accept the blame

Basically, here you take a passive role, throwing yourself on the mercy of the court (or the boss).

Accept the criticism, then move things along to another topic

If the critics are rational, the best thing may be to listen to what they have to say, acknowledge your mistakes, then try to nudge the discussion along. It may take less time and energy, and less of your political capital, to resist the impulse to explain or defend why you did what you did. (See below for ideas on how to defend, when you must.)

Probe the criticism and "mine" the good ideas

In this approach, you go beyond simply hearing out the critics. Instead, take an *active* role by asking questions and digging deeper into the ideas behind what you're hearing.

Ask questions like, "What signals do you think I missed?," or, "If this comes up again, how do you suggest I handle it?"

- When you probe the critics, the answers that come back may yield good ideas and insights both on this project, as well as on how you are perceived by others.

- By probing, you get a better understanding not only of the criticism, but also of *why that person is making it*. Are they saying this for a sound reason, based on experience? Or because of personal animosity? Or to make you look bad?

- When you take this kind of active role in probing the criticism, you may be able to turn the tables on your critics. If they have spoken up only to criticize, and are unable to come up with any positive solutions when asked, then both they and their criticism, lose credibility.

Defend, as necessary.

Sometimes you must defend yourself in order to keep your job or your reputation.

But before moving into a defensive mode, be absolutely sure you understand the criticism and why it is being made

Probe. Listen well. Ask questions, particularly on how they would have done things differently *under the circumstances as they existed at the time you had to act.*

Bringing the discussion back to the real-world situation *as it was at that time* may be the best way of defending. They may realize that, given things as they were then, and given the options available at that time, then may well have done the same as you.

If appropriate, rephrase the criticism as a way of defusing or deflating it.

Example: *"Are you saying that you would never, under any circumstances, have made the decision to_____?"*

Put the criticism into context.

Maybe the criticism has grown out of proportion. Maybe the discussion has centered on one minor aspect. If so, say something on the order of, *"What I seem to be hearing is that we are in general accord on the plan, and that the disagreement is confined to this one point? Am I correct on that?"*

Then move on to your next point, without letting the discussion bog down.

Distinguish between the point of the criticism and your actual position.

Example: *"I totally agree with you that _____. However, what I was actually suggesting was that _____."*

Answer the criticism.

In this approach, you hold to the position you took as the best under the circumstances at the time. Or as the most logical choice. *"I do understand the point you're making, and I can tell you that we did consider that. However, in the end, we elected to make the choice we did because _____."*

Checklist: When you're being criticized for a past decision or action

Note: you can use this checklist as a tool for "getting on the same side of the table" as your critic. That is, instead of defending, use the questions to gain agreement on what might have earlier been points of agreement.

- What—back at that time—were we trying to accomplish? Did we accomplish all or part of that? If yes, then it was not altogether a failure.

- Were we (I and the person who's now criticizing me) back then in accord on those objectives? If there were multiple objectives, were we in accord on which was highest priority?

- Are we still in accord that this was the right objective? If not, why not? What has changed?

- Given the circumstances at the time, what other choices did I (or we) in fact have? (Circumstances may include resources such as money, cooperation of others, time, even what was known and unknown at that time.) Was it the right choice then—given the situation as it was, and what we knew?

14.7   What learning can I draw from this experience?

In deriving learning from both your setbacks and successes, consider questions like those in this checklist below. Add additional questions from your own experience.

- In this situation, was my objective in fact as clear as it could have been? Did I have a clear sense of what I was trying to accomplish?

- Did the other parties (particularly my boss or client) also have clear objectives?

- Did I know and understand those objectives?

- Should I have taken the initiative to work with them in clarifying their objective?

- Should I have taken more of an initiative to define our differences, and to find common ground?

- Based on this success or setback, should I modify my future approaches?

- Did I in fact lack the necessary experience, skills, or connections? How can I acquire what I need?

- If I lack that experience, skills or whatever, should I make the effort to acquire them? Or should I just recognize that I can't master everything, and next time leave it to others?

- Did the outcome suggest that this is an area in which I have strengths that I didn't previously realize? (Maybe a knack for negotiating that you had never tapped.) Did it indicate this is an area where I lack real interest or aptitude? What implications?

- Did I handle the "people aspects" well (that is, areas such as interpersonal relations, communications, "political," and the like)? What should I work on for next time?

- Overall, is it really a good idea for me to continue down this pathway? Would it be best to try to avoid this kind of work or situation in the future? Or should I develop this as a new area of potential?

- Did I let myself get drawn into making too large an investment of time or energy? Could I have better used that time, energy, and other resources in accomplishing other, more important goals?

- If this outcome was disappointing, is there a larger lesson? Perhaps there was no need or no market for what I was offering. Or is the lesson that I failed to communicate effectively, or to build an awareness of the other parties' needs for what I proposed?

Summary

Question 14

What should I be considering afterward? What lessons did I learn from this?

14.1   What was I trying to accomplish here? Looking back, Was that the correct objective? To what extent did I succeed? To what extent did I fail?

14.2   Did I get value from this? Did I *give* real value?

14.3   What should I do differently—or the same—if I encounter this kind of situation again?

14.4   Suppose I had the chance to do this all over again . . .

14.5   IS there a way I can go back and remake that decision? BUT, would that be worth the costs? AND what other new opportunities would I be sacrificing?

14.6   If I hear (or anticipate) criticism on this, what is likely to be the best response in this situation?

14.7   What learning can I draw from this experience?

Question 15

What's the best choice under these circumstances? Is this a decision I can defend?

> *"Some managers tend to be frightened of decisions because they are concerned with making an error. The important thing to remember is that the company can run with some bad decisions, but it definitely cannot run with no decisions."*
>
> Corporate CEO

Some of us find it scary to make decisions. It's actually very easy to make decisions: Just flip a coin, or throw a dart, or go with gut feel . . . and at least some of the time you'll end up with an OK outcome.

Ah, but, there is a catch. When you make decisions by flipping a coin or going on gut feel, you'll find it hard to persuade others that this really is the best choice. They'll second-guess you, they'll nit-pick, they'll argue over ends and means. In the end, they may decline to go along with your decision.

Even worse, even you may not be confident that you really made the right move. You'll wonder and worry and stay awake nights making and remaking your call.

"But I don't make decisions; I just carry out decisions made by my boss."

It may *seem* that you have no role in the decision-making. But that's generally not the reality:

> *"Usually the manager or executive who professes to have no decision making authority is in fact constantly making*

decision—though unfortunately these are often made by default, by passing the buck to a superior or committee."

Corporate Vice-president

The realities of decisions

The first reality is that often *no "perfect"* decision exists. Instead, there is only the *best available choice*, given the circumstances of facts, time-frame and resources at hand.

Second reality: no matter what you decide (or recommend to an upper-level decision maker) you'll always need to be prepared to "sell" that recommendation or suggestion.

If you're recommending a choice to your boss or upper levels, you'll need to be ready to set the context regarding the situation and the choices, and why you are convinced that the option you recommend is the best choice available.

You may also need to respond to the concerns of your boss, but may also need to be prepared to defend it against nitpickers in the ranks: Maybe your game-playing peers want to throw you off stride, either to gain an advantage, or to prevent your recommendation from going through (and impinging on their turf, staff, or budget).

Even if you're the only one impacted by this decision, then it's no less important to be able to sell that choice to yourself later—maybe when you're second-guessing yourself some sleepless night.

So how *do* you make decisions that you can be confident in defending to your boss as the best choice under the circumstances?

How do you arrive at positions that you can defend when you're presenting to skeptical people with different ideas on what's best— and with different perceptions of what they think are the facts?

How do you make choices that you trust enough so you don't feel compelled to go back and second-guess?

I find four key questions helpful both in making sound decisions, and in defending them:

- What are we **ultimately trying to accomplish** *here*, and how will we recognize that we've been successful?

- What **practical, realistic ways of achieving that end** are open to us?

- How do these **alternatives compare?**

- Which of these alternatives **best achieves our desired outcome**, with **the fewest adverse consequences**?

Let's look in more detail at each of these questions.

15.1 What are we ultimately trying to accomplish here? That is, "Where" do we want or need to be afterwards?

This echoes some of the questions at the start of this book. (You may want to flip back to Question 1 for a quick refresher.)

- What is our ultimate objective? "Where" do we want to be when it's all finished? What problems are we trying to solve here? How will we recognize that we have been successful?

- Who else is involved? What is likely to be their objective? (That is, what problems are they likely to be trying to solve, and how will they recognize that they have been successful?)

The point is that in order to arrive at a sensible decision that you can defend to others, or against your own later second-guessing, it is important to determine both:

- What that decision is to accomplish for you; as well as,

- Who else may have a stake in that decision, and what they likely want to accomplish.

Granted, you may not know who is involved or what they likely want, at least not at the start. Nonetheless, by giving early thought to what other partiers may have an interest in this, you get started on the process of arriving at an outcome that "works" for all, and that you can defend if it becomes necessary.

15.2 What practical, realistic ways of achieving that end are open to us? That is, What realistic options are open to us here?

You go to a restaurant, the waiter shows you to a table, and says, *"We have ze boeuf bourguignonne. Oui ou non?"*

Your response would probably be something like, "Well, that sounds nice but what are the other choices? I'd like to see the menu, *s'il vous plait.*"

We look for the menu before making a choice in a restaurant, but in the rest of life too often get drawn into making yes-no choices on the first idea that comes to mind.

And then what happens? Maybe we make a decision, and then, only after we're locked in, realize, "What were we thinking? There were other, better alternatives! If only we'd taken the time to think it through!"

Setting up the "option menu"

What should be on the decision menu?

First are the "always" options: *Do nothing at all*, and *Wait before acting*.

Why "always?" Because doing nothing, or waiting before making a move, may be the *worst* possible thing to do.

Conversely, doing nothing at all, or doing nothing for a while, may actually be the *best* choice.

No matter, these "always" options are *always* worth considering: If they work out to be good options then you can go from there. But you can never know for sure until you explore what flows from them.

If they prove to be worthless, then you can cross them off and move on with the way clear, and have no temptation to dither and dilly-dally.

First "always" option: Consciously elect to do nothing at all.

"Do nothing at all" is an option that should always be considered. Doing nothing, just letting events run their course, sometimes is a very good thing to do. Other times it's not good. Hence it's prudent to think through, early on, whether inaction is best in this case.

Second always option: Consciously choose to wait before making any choice or any move.

That first option, "Do nothing," means deciding to take no action, now or later. "Waiting before acting" means holding off, pausing to see what develops, before making a choice, or acting on that choice.

Adding to the option menu

Once you've listed those two "always" options, then add alternatives that are specific to this situation.

Sometimes these other possibilities will be apparent. Nevertheless, it's prudent to do some more research, even if that research consists of nothing more than talking it over with other people.

And be creative, perhaps by coming up with all-new possibilities, or by combining elements of other alternatives, creating fresh approaches from the existing.

At this stage, concentrate on *adding* possibilities, not eliminating them. If it might just be a reasonable possible way of achieving that most desired outcome, then include it. There will be time—and a tool—for editing out later.

What makes an option a "reasonable" possibility, worth adding to the menu, depends on the circumstances. At this point, err on the side of inclusion.

First column of the decision making template

From this point, we'll be pulling these factors into a template for making sense of the facts, as well as the array of options, and of course the consequences that flow from each option. The first part of that template is vertical:

Options
Do nothing at all
Wait before acting or deciding
Your specific option #1
Your specific option #2

15.3 How do these alternatives compare on the key relevant measures?

On what basis should you compare the alternatives?

To some extent, that will depend on the specific situation you face, but there are five considerations that always need to consider as you examine each of those menu items:

Important: In setting up these alternatives to compare, keep in mind that you are also setting up your structure for presenting your recommendation to others . . . or for reassuring yourself later that you arrived at the best possible choice.

Advantages.

What makes this alternative seem like a good idea? What could you gain from choosing it? How does it help achieve the objective you set?

Disadvantages.

What works against this item?

Costs.

Normally, this will relate to dollar costs as well as costs in time or inconvenience. But think of these as direct items—costs (in whatever form) that you will "spend" now, rather than later.

Indirect consequences.

Suppose you choose Option A. What impacts will that likely bring about later, down the line? For example, If you choose the option "Buy a new car now," then there will be *immediate costs*, but there will also be *indirect consequences* later, such as your cash or credit is lowered for things you may need to buy another time. Or, if you choose this option, what would the longer-term effects be—such as alienating someone you would later want as a friend or ally?

Personal preferences.

Hunches, intuitions, and "gut feel" are all valid inputs that should be factored into any significant decision. If something doesn't "feel right" to you, better pay attention to that, because subconscious ways of knowing are sometimes even more accurate than any kind of logical thinking or "hard" research. How much weight you give to these preferences and hunches is up to you, but do let them come to the surface so you can act on them in a conscious way.

Any other considerations to factor in?

Add any other factors that are relevant to this particular situation. For example, if time is a factor, then how quickly each option could be implemented would be noted here.

Template for organizing your decision

The template that you'll find a couple of pages ahead is a tool for pulling all of these considerations together into a unified overview so you can see the options and relevant factors at a glance. (This template can also serve as a tool if you are making a presentation to the boss or others. You can unveil the options and the conseq1uences that flow from them item by item.).

15.4 Which of these alternatives will best achieve the goal, with the fewest adverse consequences?

The template helps you sort out how the various alternatives compare against the criteria of

- Advantages,

- Disadvantages,

- Short term costs,

- Indirect (longer-term) consequences, and your

- Personal Preferences.

Add any other criteria specific to the particular situation you face.

The template does not *make* the decision for you; it only helps to set out and organize the data, so you can *compare* the reasonable alternatives that exist, and compare what likely consequences will flow from each.

Once all that is clear, once you have a sense of the advantages, disadvantages, likely costs and consequences of each option, *then* it is time to make the choice.

Choose on what basis? By looking at the alternatives and answering this question: Which best achieves the most desired objective you defined earlier, with the *fewest adverse consequences*?

Notice that the right question is *not*, Which is the best alternative? but rather, Which best gets you "where" you want or need to be?

For example, that sleek convertible you could buy at a fraction of book value might be the *best alternative* (if you're into cars). But a sporty car, no matter how good the deal, is not going to be the best way of achieving your objective of transportation to your remote mountain cabin.

Options	Advantages	Disadvantages
Do nothing at all		
Wait before acting or deciding		
Your specific option #1		
Your specific option #2		

Direct, present costs	Indirect / later consequences	Personal preferences	Other

Double-checking your proposed decision

Most of the time, you'll likely be satisfied that you have settled on the best choice available, and that you can defend that decision, either to others or to yourself later.

Nonetheless, here are three additional supplemental "double-check" questions that you may want to consider.

15.5 Double-check: Key consideration in making the decision: Does it pass the "feel right" test?

We focus on the analytical, logical side of decision making in the template above.

Logic and analysis are important in making sound decisions—but no less important are our intuitions, experiences, and just general "feelings."

We factored some of them in on the final column of that template, but before locking in on a decision, it's wise to draw back and just take a reading of how that selection *feels* to you.

No matter how logical the choice may seem, if it doesn't feel comfortable to you, if something about it nags at you, then—just maybe—the analysis is wrong, or doesn't fit.

Or maybe the analysis is okay, but you've set yourself up to pursue the wrong objective.

Checklist: the "feel right" test

- Does it in fact "feel" right to me? Or is there something about it that troubles me, maybe in a way I can't put my finger on?

- Is it a choice that will "fit" with the various personalities involved?

- Am I committed enough to it to be honestly convincing when working with others?

- Can I stand behind it as the best choice, given the circumstances as they are (or were) at the time I made that choice?

- How confident am I that I will, in the future, be glad I settled on this choice?

15.6 Double-check: If it is difficult to choose among alternative goals, ask,

- **Which potential goal has priority?**

- **Why that goal over the other possibilities?**

- **Is there a way we can gain the best parts of all?**

When you sort out the situation, you may find that there are conflicting goals, and those conflicts are at the heart of why you're finding it hard to make the final decision.

Checklist: selecting among competing goals

In selecting among conflicting objectives, consider factors such as these below, but add others specific to your actual situation:

- Which offers the highest payoff if I am successful in accomplishing it?

- Which entails the greatest risk? Least risk?

- Which has highest costs—both indirect and direct?

- Which, in my present judgment, seems most likely to work out best in the longer term?

- Which offers the prospect of the best and smoothest relations with other people and departments?

Use the template below as a model for structuring and balancing those varied concerns. Again, add any other criteria that are relevant to the specific situation.

Criteria	Potential goal A	Potential goal B	Potential goal C
Highest payoff if successful?			
Greatest risk? Least risk?			
Highest costs— direct or hidden?			
Which do you think/feel is likely to work out best?			
Offers best relations with others (fewest hard feelings, etc.)?			
Add other specific criteria			

15.7 Double-check: What assumptions have I made? What best-guesses have I been forced to make about presently-unknown or unknowable factors? What impacts would they have, in both best-case and worst-case turn of events?

Sometimes, maybe even most of the time, we have to make choices even though things are less than ideal. There might not be quite enough funding, not quite enough help or expertise. We might not have full knowledge of all the facts, let alone what unexpected events may come along.

Sometimes there are no good alternatives from which to choose, so we have to select from a bad menu.

The point is, we don't always have the luxury of trying to decide among "perfect" options. Sometimes there are no perfect, maybe not even fairly good alternatives. Sometimes we have to decide based on what is *available* now, and what we *know* now.

Example: your old car is giving trouble, and you're wondering whether to replace it.

One assumption you might be making is that you will follow through on your plan to attend evening classes at the university's main campus over the winter. That assumption plays a key role in choosing whether to invest in a really secure car for winter driving. But what if your assumption is wrong, and those courses are cancelled?

Another assumption might be that gas prices stay around the present level, so you can predict driving costs.

Still another assumption might be that you keep your present job, which would mean, first, that you have enough spare cash to pay for a car; and, second, that you won't be moving into a new job where you might be too overworked to think of commuting downstate to classes.

Checklist: what unknowns and what-ifs lurk?

- What can go wrong, cost more, take longer, get lost, break, or whatever? How serious would that be?

- How can we prepare for any unknowns? (In the jargon, What's our contingency plan? Or, What is Plan B?)

- What unknowns might go better than anticipated? With what effect?

- What factors might go worse than anticipated? With what effect?

Summary

Question 15

What's the best choice under these circumstances? Is this a decision I can defend?

15.1   What are we ultimately trying to accomplish here? That is, "Where" do we want or need to be afterwards?

15.2   What practical, realistic ways of achieving that end are open to us? That is, What realistic options are open to us here?

15.3   How do these alternatives compare on the key relevant measures?

15.4   Which of these alternatives will best achieve the goal, with the fewest adverse consequences?

15.5   Double-check: Key consideration in making the decision: Does it pass the "feel right" test?

15.6   Double-check: If it is difficult to choose among alternative goals, ask,

15.7   Double-check: What assumptions have I made? What best-guesses have I been forced to make about presently-unknown or unknowable factors? What impacts would they have, in both best-case and worst-case turn of events?

Question 16

If I were to look back on this later. . .

You've heard of post-mortem analysis. Whatever it was is over and done with, and now you are trying to find what went wrong, what killed it. Or what made it go particularly well.

The military has a similar protocol, the "After-action Report": an unblinking look at what went wrong and right, and what can be learned from it next time.

Ignatius Loyola, founder of the Jesuit order (himself a former soldier) developed his *Spiritual Exercises*. One of the exercises for people undergoing retreats was to visualize themselves on their death-bed, asking,

> *"What, as I lay dying, will I most regret, and what can I do about that now, before it's too late?"*

Here are some questions to help in that post-mortem analysis.

16.1 Suppose, at some time in the future, I look back on this: Would I be more likely to regret *doing* this, or *failing* to try it?

Jeff Bezos, founder and CEO of Amazon, was cited in an article in *The Economist*:

> *" . . . in the 1990s [Bezos] hesitated to leave a good job in the world of finance to set up Amazon after a colleague had advised him against it. But Bezos applied what he calls a 'regret minimalization framework', imagining whether, as*

an 80 year-old looking back, he would regret the decision not to strike out on his own."

As we all know, especially if you're reading this in e-book form on an Amazon Kindle, Bezos *did* choose to give it a try.

A further benefit: Once he had done his "regret minimalization" analysis, he could feel free to plunge in full force, with no qualms hesitations, and second-thoughts.

16.2   What would a "Pre-mortem analysis" tell me?

David Ignatius, columnist for the *Washington Post* and a first-rank writer of knowledgeable, intelligent political/economic thrillers, wrote this, referring to events at the World Economic Forum at Davos, Switzerland:

> *"One of the most powerful ideas heard at Davos was the idea of 'pre-mortem' analysis . . . A pre-mortem analysis can provide a real 'stress test' to conventional thinking. Let's say that a company or a government agency has decided on a plan of action. But before implementing it, the boss asks people to assume that five years from now, the plan has failed—and then to write a brief explanation of why it didn't work.*

> *"The approach stands a chance of bringing to the surface problems that the decision makers had overlooked—the 'black swans,' to use . . .[Nassim Nicholas Taleb's phrase, title of a book he wrote, relating to events] that people assumed wouldn't happen in the near future because they hadn't occurred in the recent past."*

The point? Now, before all is locked in, it would be very wise for you to do a flash-forward exercise modeled on one of these, asking yourself whatever form of these questions works best for you:

Ignatius Loyola: What, when all is said and done, will I wish I had done differently on this matter?

Jeff Bezos: "Regret minimization framework"—Later on, will I most regret that I did, or did not, give this a try?

David Ignatius, the financial gnomes of the Davos Forum, and the concept of "pre-mortem analysis": Let's imagine we could flash-forward to the future on this, and let's also pretend this project failed: Why did it fail? Was there something we failed to anticipate and prepare for? Was there something we could have done differently?

Bottom line: project your mind forward, as if to some time in the future, a time when the consequences are locked in, and ask, When I look back on this situation , what would I . . .

- *Wish I had done* at this point?

- *Regret* that I had done at this point?

- Regret that I *failed to do* at this point?

Summary

Question 16

If I were to look back on this in the future . . .

16.1   Suppose, at some time in the future, I look back on this: Would I be more likely to regret *doing* this, or *failing* to try it?

16.2   What would a "Pre-mortem analysis" tell me?

Overview checklist: The Smart Questions

Part one

WHAT IS THIS "GAME" ABOUT?

Question 1

How do I (my team) "win"? That is, "Where" do we want or need to be afterward, and how will we recognize that we've arrived there?

1.1   Is this where I ULTIMATELY need to arrive? Or is there something I need even more than that? That is, is this in fact the desired END, or just a MEANS to that end?

1.2   On what time-frame am I working: short, mid, or long-term?

1.3   Given that time and resources are always finite, why this over all other possibilities?

1.4   What elements do I NEED as part of this goal? What elements do I NOT want, or are not essential?

1.5   Suppose I DO accomplish this, then what?

1.6   Is pursuing this really how I want to be spending my energy, creativity, and time? If not, what can I do to change the situation?

1.7   Check: Is this something that really matters, or am I going for it for trivial reasons, such as to make a report or resume look better?

1.8   If you find it difficult to choose among alternative possible goals, which has ultimate priority? Why?

Question 2

Who else is involved in this "game"? What is likely to be their idea of "winning"?

2.1   Who are the other "players"—directly or indirectly? Why? What is their involvement?

2.2   How does each of these "players" win? That is, what problem are they likely trying to solve, and how will they measure success?

2.3   What are the other "players" rewarded for, or punished for? What implications result?

Question 3

What's really going on here? Is this a real issue, or a subtle test?

3.1   Is this really *just* a coincidence? Or is it a subtle test?

3.2   Are they trying to manipulate me? What are they really after?

3.3   Is this a dominance test? Is it a "red-flag" test?

3.4   What's really going on in this meeting?

Question 4

What is this situation ultimately about? Where is the "crunch"?

4.1   Is this a real conflict over real things? Or is it just a matter of some personalities getting crosswise with each other?

4.2   Is this conflict (or looming conflict) really about the present situation, or is it about something from the past or future?

Part two

HOW AM I DOING SO FAR?

Question 5

Am I being given the recognition and compensation that I *honestly* deserve? If not, why not?

5.1   Where do the significant dollars go in my organization, profession, or trade? To whom or to what group? Why there?

5.2   Is another person (or another department, etc.) getting the rewards, promotions, budget, etc. that should go to me? Who? Why? What can I do?

5.3   If I am not getting the recognition and pay that my work— honestly— deserves, why not?

5.4   Who are the important judges? How do they view me and my work? What implications?

Question 6

Am I attuned to the "real rules" that operate here? Is "disinformation" part of the way of life?

6.1   What are the professed "articles of faith" here? Does the reality differ?

6.2   Is a secret, coded "quasi-language" used here?

Question 7

Am I focusing my time and efforts on the ends that matter most?

7.1   In assessing whether you are focusing your time and efforts on the ends that matter most, ask,

7.2   Are there productive ways in which I can expand my contribution?

7.3   Given the real-world limits of time and resources that exist here, what should I *not* be doing now. . . or at least not as priority?

7.4   Is what I am doing now (both at this particular moment and overall) genuinely constructive, or am I just keeping busy?

7.5   If I were doing this work as a self-employed entrepreneur, not an employee, what would I do differently?

Question 8

Am I learning from the right role models?

8.1   Who are the people generally recognized as outstanding in my organization or profession? Why? What does that suggest?

8.2   Suppose these outstanding people now held my role or job: What would they do differently than I? The same? Why?

8.3   What specific, practical action steps will I take in adopting these new methods into my own approach?

Question 9

Am I engineering the conditions that lead to success? Or am I setting up for failure?

9.1   Do I choose the right targets? Do I choose achievable goals?

9.2   Do I engineer conditions around myself and my work in ways that increase the probability and frequency of my experiencing success?

9.3   Do I recognize—and draw strength and confidence from— my successes?

9.4   Have I developed the mind-set of converting problems into challenges?

9.5   Do I move rapidly through my setbacks—AND my lukewarm partial successes—in order to find my real successes? Do I recognize when to cut my losses and move on?

9.6   If I am not committed to this project, why don't I just cut my losses and get out now, freeing myself to find something to which I can give 100%?

Question 10

Am I willing to trade my comfortable set of self-fulfilling expectations of limited success for more productive expectations that push me to risk and grow?

10.1   Do I dare to extend my limits, and take the risk of setbacks?

10.2   Do I dare to take risks . . . but *expect* to succeed?

10.3   Do I put my energy into being productive, not just into avoiding failure?

10.4   Do I understand—deep down inside—that I'm not the only one here feeling a sense of insecurity? Do I push on, regardless?

Part three:

WHAT'S MY BEST MOVE AT THIS POINT?

Question 11

Is a confrontation really necessary? If yes, is this the best time and place?

11.1   Is a conflict taking place, overtly or covertly? What is it really about?

11.2   Will going into a conflict mode here and now really help me accomplish my ultimate objective?

11.3   Suppose I "win" this conflict—what do I gain? Suppose I "lose"—what likely consequences, both immediate and longer-term?

11.4   If the conflict is both real and significant, is now in fact the best time to deal with it?

11.5   Is this a situation in which it's best to accept a strategic defeat—that is, to lose gracefully now, in order to be better positioned for the future?

Question 12

Do I really need to be involved in this? Is this really *my* problem? If yes, is now the best time?

12.1   Whose problem IS it? Am I necessarily involved?

12.2   Is this really a problem that I (or we) should be investing time and effort in solving? If yes, is now the right time?

12.3   Check: Is what I am proposing to do (or say) likely to help resolve (rather than complicate) the issue?

12.4   Is there a practical, realistic way that I can—right now—cut through to bring the issue to some kind of closure?

Question 13

What should I consider before taking action? Am I thinking enough steps ahead?

13.1   In this situation, what moves might I make? How would each of these potential moves likely play out down the line?

13.2   What unknowns and vulnerabilities lurk here? How can I prepare for and correct for them now?

13.3   What mistakes am I at risk of making?

13.4   What other games may be in play here?

13.5   Whose input/advice/"buy-in" might I later wish I had gotten?

13.6   Are any broader opportunities hidden within this situation?

13.7   If it's such good idea, why hasn't somebody already done it . and gotten rich?

13.8   How can I make it "bulletproof?"

13.9   Can I "monetize" it?

Question 14

What should I be considering afterward? What lessons did I learn from this?

14.1   What was I trying to accomplish here? Looking back, Was that the correct objective? To what extent did I succeed? To what extent did I fail?

14.2   Did I get value from this? Did I *give* real value?

14.3   What should I do differently—or the same—if I encounter this kind of situation again?

14.4   Suppose I had the chance to do this all over again . . .

14.5   IS there a way I can go back and remake that decision? BUT, would that be worth the costs? AND what other new opportunities would I be sacrificing?

14.6   If I hear (or anticipate) criticism on this, what is likely to be the best response in this situation?

14.7   What learning can I draw from this experience?

Question 15

What's the best choice under these circumstances? Is this a decision I can defend?

15.1   What are we ultimately trying to accomplish here? That is, "Where" do we want or need to be afterwards?

15.2   What practical, realistic ways of achieving that end are open to us? That is, What realistic options are open to us here?

15.3 How do these alternatives compare on the key relevant measures?

15.4 Which of these alternatives will best achieve the goal, with the fewest adverse consequences?

15.5 Double-check: Key consideration in making the decision: Does it pass the "feel right" test?

15.6 Double-check: If it is difficult to choose among alternative goals, ask,

15.7 Double-check: What assumptions have I made? What best-guesses have I been forced to make about presently-unknown or unknowable factors? What impacts would they have, in both best-case and worst-case turn of events?

Question 16

If I were to look back on this later . . .

16.1 Suppose, at some time in the future, I look back on this: Would I be more likely to regret *doing* this, or *failing* to try it?

16.2 What would a "Pre-mortem analysis" tell me?

About the author

Michael McGaulley, J.D., is a lawyer and management consultant. He is a graduate of the Cornell Law School, admitted to practice in New York, Virginia, and the District of Columbia.

His consulting clients have included the Foreign Service Institute of the U.S. State Department, various other federal departments in both the civilian and military sectors, and private companies such as Xerox in the United States, Canada, and Europe; Bank of America; Kodak, and others. This work gave him the chance to see how organizations and the individuals within operate on both the visible and sub-surface levels.

In addition to this book, *How to Ask the Smart Questions for Wining the Games of Business and Life*, he is the author of an upcoming book on subtle communication skills, next in this Career Development Series.

He has also written a series of how-to guides on consultative selling skills for entrepreneurs, free agents, consultants, and professional sales people.

His other books include the novel, *Joining Miracles,* and the technothrillers *A Remedy for Death*, and *The Grail Conspiracies.*

His blogs and websites include

- CareerSuccessHow-to.com

- MichaelMcGaulley.net

The books in the Career Savvy People Skills Series:

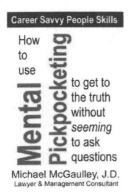

Career Savvy People Skills

How to use **Mental Pickpocketing** to get to the truth without *seeming* to ask questions

Michael McGaulley, J.D.
Lawyer & Management Consultant

How to use MENTAL PICKPOCKETING to get to the truth without seeming to ask questions

When you ask a question, *most* of the time, *most* people will do their best to tell the truth, But not always. Sometimes simply to ask a question is to give the game away because it alerts the other person to what you're really after, and hence raises a flag on what they may want to fudge, avoid, or distort. (Or even tell a fib!) *Mental Pickpocketing* introduces you to an array of methods of getting to the truth without seeming to ask questions.   To order via Amazon

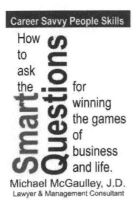

Career Savvy People Skills

How to ask the **Smart Questions** for winning the games of business and life.

Michael McGaulley, J.D.
Lawyer & Management Consultant

How to ask the SMART QUESTIONS for winning the games of career and life

"You've got to be aware of the games that are being played. You don't have to play the games yourself, but you do need to recognize when they are being played against you." Like it or not, the reality is that games, probes, and subtle competitions—and not to forget office politics! —are facts of life in most organizations. *Smart Questions* provides the tools for looking through to what's really going on in situations, on spotting the "real rules", on focusing on what really matters and staying out of unnecessary confrontations, and on selecting the best option under the circumstances—and defending it if challenged.   To order via Amazon

Legal and copyright notices continued from the front of this book

The materials contained in this e-book and related website are provided for general information purposes only and do not constitute legal or other professional advice on any subject matter. Neither the author nor publisher accept any responsibility for any loss which may arise from reliance on information contained in this book or related website.

Some links within this e-book or related website may lead to other websites, including those operated and maintained by third parties. The author and publisher of this e-book include these links solely as a convenience to you, and the presence of such a link does not imply a responsibility for the linked site or an endorsement of the linked site, its operator, or its contents.

The publisher and author accept no liability whatsoever for any losses or damages caused or alleged to be caused, directly or indirectly, by utilization of any information contained herein, or obtained from any of the persons or entities herein above.

This book and related website and its contents are provided "AS IS" without warranty of any kind, either express or implied, including, but not limited to, the implied warranties of merchantability, fitness for a particular purpose, or non-infringement.

If you, or any other reader, do not agree to these policies as noted above, please do not use these materials or any services offered herein.

Your use of these materials indicates acceptance of these policies.

This book is intellectual property. No part of this publication may be stored in a retrieval system, transmitted or reproduced in any way, including but not limited to digital copying and printing without the prior agreement and written permission of the author and publisher.

Made in the USA
Middletown, DE
03 July 2018